Saying "I Do"

THE WEDDING CEREMONY

*The Complete Guide
to a Perfect Wedding*

Steven M. Neel

W0010065

MERIWETHER PUBLISHING LTD.
Colorado Springs, Colorado

Meriwether Publishing Ltd., Publisher
P.O. Box 7710
Colorado Springs, CO 80933

Editor: Rhonda Wray
Typesetting: Sharon E. Garlock
Cover design: Tom Myers
Cover and inside photography: Kathy Halstead Barnes

The Old and New Testament quotations in this publication are from The New King James Version. Copyright © 1979, 1980, 1982, Thomas Nelson, Inc.

Selections from Tobit and Sirach are taken from the *New American Bible*. Copyright © 1970 Confraternity of Christian Doctrine, Washington, DC. Used with permission. All rights reserved.

Library of Congress Cataloging-in-Publication Data

Neel, Steven M., 1947-
    Saying "I do" : the wedding ceremony / by Steven M. Neel. --1st ed.
      p.   c.m.
    ISBN 1-56608-012-6
    1. Wedding etiquette. I. Title.
  BJ2051.N378   1995
  395'.22--dc20   95-31890
                                                    CIP

DEDICATION

This book is dedicated to my wife, Carmen Alanis Neel, whose love, encouragement, patience, and editorial contributions made this effort possible. Without her firm prodding and moral support, I would never have completed this book.

Contents

Preface

Let me tell you a few things about this wedding ceremony planning guide. What you are about to read has evolved through many years of experience, observation, and research. It is an attempt to share some insights I have gained in order to make your wedding ceremony planning easy, enjoyable, and meaningful. It leads you through the planning process. It allows you, as a couple, to thoroughly examine your options, explore topics that you might not have considered, and to be confident that you are making the right choices for yourselves. Familiarize yourself with its contents and take advantage of the help it provides. Wedding ceremony planning can be hectic, nerve-racking, and frustrating work, but it doesn't have to be.

As an ordained minister for more than eighteen years, I have found that couples who approach me to perform their wedding have consulted standard wedding planners and are well-versed in reception planning, announcement/invitation etiquette, and apparel. However, there are so many things vying for their attention and so many choices to make that few of them have given serious thought to the long-term roles and responsibilities of the marriage relationship or the near-term wedding ceremony itself. As a result, our initial interview meeting often consists of questioning stares when I ask the couple why they want to get married, what their plans are for their life together, and what type of ceremony they desire.

Consequently, over time I compiled a patchwork of information into a handout that I give to couples during our initial interview meeting to take home. This information is designed to stimulate thought and discussion and to provide a basis for more productive follow-up premarital counseling meetings. Through encouragement from fellow ministers, I have expanded that original handout material into this comprehensive planning guide.

This planning guide concentrates specifically on helping you plan your wedding ceremony. It is a thorough, accurate, and practical guide designed to help you prepare for one of the most exciting and significant events of your lives.

In an attempt to make the ceremony planner usable to a broad audience, I have included material on ceremonies of various major religions in the United States, as well as some denominational variances. Realizing that I am limited by my religious background, education, and experience, I had this material reviewed by representatives of various religions.

There are many fine wedding planners on the market that provide valuable information on the full spectrum of activities surrounding the ceremony. I encourage you to get one and use it. But this wedding ceremony planning guide is unique because it focuses on those events directly associated with the wedding ceremony. This information is important and is not included in other currently available, general wedding planners. As such, this wedding ceremony planning guide does not compete with, but is a companion to, the other wedding planners.

It is my hope that future editions of this book will be as helpful as I have tried to make this edition. Please write to me via Meriwether Publishing Ltd. with information on topics that I have omitted (such as cultural traditions), to provide additional information on topics that are included, and/or to offer suggestions to make this guide more practical. Your letters will be directed to me, and I will use the information to revise the text for each new edition. When requested, credit will be given to the source.

Thank you in advance for your interest and participation in making this the best possible book on wedding planning.

The Reverend Steven M. Neel, D.D.

Acknowledgments

When writing a manuscript such as this, one tends to focus in a particular direction, overlook some facts, make inadvertent errors, forget to include some material, or simply be unaware of some information.

Realizing my own religious, educational, and experience limitations, I turned to the following people to review the manuscript and provide corrections, additions, and/or clarifications to make the material more complete. I greatly appreciate their assistance and stand in their debt. God bless them.

Reverend Father John Asimacopoulos
St. Nicholas Greek Orthodox Church
Greek Orthodox Archdiocese of North and South America
San Jose, California

Reverend Mark Brocker
St. Paul's Lutheran Church
Franklin Grove, Illinois

Narendra Kumar, Temple Administrator
Vedic Dharma Samaj
Hindu Temple and Cultural Center
Fremont, California

Joe and Emily LaScola
Family Life Ministry
Diocese of San Jose
San Jose, California

Reverend Edward Richards
Valley Community Church
San Jose, California

Dr. Khalid Siddiqi, Director
Islamic Education and Information Center
San Jose, California

Several friends read this manuscript and generously made many suggestions to improve it. I acknowledge with deep appreciation and special thanks the patience, insight, and support of Kim Carney, Richard J. Helley, Rosa Lee Pagliaro, and Karen Robinson in the tedious task of reviewing and editing my work. These talented people spent countless hours painstakingly editing and re-editing the material and making invaluable corrections and suggestions. I am gratefully indebted to them.

Publisher's Acknowledgment

The publisher wishes to express appreciation to Kathy Halstead Barnes for generously allowing her beautiful wedding photographs to be featured throughout this book.

$\mathcal{H}$elp!

(INTRODUCTION)

Congratulations! You have made, or are seriously considering, one of the most significant decisions of your lives — to get married. Whether this is your first time or whether you have been married before, that simple "yes" opens a myriad of new challenges and opportunities. As the initial emotional glow starts to wane, you begin to realize that there are a lot of decisions to make as you plan both for your wedding day and your marriage. Now is the time to decide what you want to do. But, with so much to do, where do you begin?

With all the excitement, you may not have given your ceremony much thought. The purpose of this guide is to help you examine your expectations, identify your options, and answer your questions concerning your wedding ceremony before you meet with your clergy/officiant. It fills your need for a step-by-step map through the maze of questions and decisions that now confront you. Most importantly, all the information, advice, and ideas in this guide are directed toward personalizing the most important event of your wedding day — the ceremony.

For the working *couple* who has limited time, this guide is designed to make your wedding ceremony planning simple and easy. It encourages you both to keep actively involved. This may be the first decision-making you have made together as an engaged couple. When the two of you have made your choices, they should then be reviewed and discussed with your clergy/officiant to let him/her know your wishes.

This guide will enable you to examine your options for tailoring a unique, interesting, beautiful, and joyous wedding ceremony. There is a wealth of information not only for the "first timers," but also for those of you who are renewing your vows or remarrying. As the number of remarriages continues to increase, the mores of our society have shifted. The fact that you have been married before does not necessarily limit your options. And, as the United States continues to be a melting pot of world cultures, you also have the opportunity to incorporate cultural traditions into your ceremony. Once you are clear and confident about what kind of wedding ceremony you want, your search for facilities and services will be faster and easier.

You are about to embark upon one of life's richest and most rewarding adventures. Marriage is one of the most significant commitments you can make in your lifetime. There is a distinction between a marriage and a wedding, however. A marriage is a bond and commitment. A wedding is a formal, public announcement of this bond.

Your wedding ceremony signifies that you have made a life-changing decision. It adds a binding dimension to your marital ties. Since I am a minister, it should not be surprising that the information on these pages centers on the wedding ceremony. Through the ceremony, you begin your married life together and start nurturing and developing a strong, loving, and mutually enriching marriage. Family and friends are invited to share the news, witness the wedding, and celebrate the union.

There are many fine wedding planners available in bookstores to provide information on the full spectrum of exhaustive activities associated with weddings. But they do not concentrate on the wedding ceremony, instead providing a broad, generalized approach to all the activities associated with getting married. They typically gloss over the wedding ceremony itself, leaving it up to you, the wedding couple, and your clergy/officiant to work out the specific details.

Even in the most traditional wedding, there is room for individuality. You should take an active role in the choices and decisions associated with your ceremony. When you do, your ceremony will truly reflect your attitude and commitment toward marriage and each other, and it will be filled with a lifetime of happy memories. Nothing can substitute for the pride you will feel when you publicly pledge your love and devotion to each other before your family and friends. But remember that the only ones that you have to please are yourselves. Make your preferences known. This is your day.

I hope you find this guide a useful and practical tool that makes your task easier during this significant and demanding planning process.

COMPUTERS AND PLANNING

Wedding planning has entered the computer age. Not only can computers help you with creating your mailing list, recording invitation responses, and logging wedding gifts, they can also help you communicate electronically with out-of-town guests and find wedding resources, i.e. clergy/officiants, florists, photographers, and sites.

For those of you who travel the Internet, the information highway has some off-ramps for wedding planning. The Internet contains an abundance of information that can help you plan for and survive your special day. Internet information services offer a convenient way to receive answers to wedding etiquette questions, find wedding services, and share information, ideas, and concerns with other couples who are going through the same confusion and stress that you are (an electronic support group). However, when working in the Internet, you need to make sure that the information you are perusing is for your locale. Once in the Internet, you may receive responses from anywhere around the country or even around the world.

Internet addresses that you may find helpful are listed in Table 1-1.

Table 1-1, Internet Wedding Information

Internet Address	Description
soc.couple.wedding	*Bulletin board for getting and giving wedding advice.*
alt.wedding	*Similar to the previous address.*
http://www.wam.umd.edu/-sek/ wedding.html	*soc.couple.wedding Worldwide Web site containing information grouped geographically and by service type.*
http://www.pep.com/pep/tws/ tws.html	*The Wedding Source provides advice, products and listings services.*
http://sequoia.picosof.com/ sprawl/weddings	*Wedding Online contains listings of wedding services.*
http://blackwidow.questar.com/ bridalnet/	*The Bridal Net offers a national bridal registry, plus information on services and honeymoon planning.*

CHAPTER 2

Where Should We Begin?

So this is it. You now have to put on paper, in some logical form, what you have been mulling over in your mind about what you want for your ceremony. Your wedding ceremony represents the convergence of numerous significant choices into a single event. This is your chance to make your ceremony the way you want it. All it takes is planning. There is no "right" ceremony that satisfies everyone. It is a personal experience. Plan it together to suit your individual style and budget.

Marriage is one of the most significant commitments that we make in our lifetime. Your wedding marks the beginning of your married life. In your wedding ceremony, you make public what you feel in your hearts. Ideally, your wedding day is one of the most important days of your life. The wedding ceremony, whether simple or ornate, is a critical part of that day. It is the sanctification of the marriage. Ideally, the ceremony and setting should be in keeping with that meaning and purpose. You should carefully plan for it as far in advance of the scheduled date as possible. But do not lose sight of whose wedding it is during the planning process. The wedding is for the two of you. Plan it together to match your dreams. Make your wedding a personal statement.

Do not be intimidated by the size of the questionnaire. It contains items for the full range of wedding types and settings so that you can think about the full options and considerations that confront you. The questionnaire covers a lot of "details" that you may not have thought of or you may have overlooked. While not every item will apply to your particular wedding desires, this questionnaire enables you to think through and/or rethink some of your notions about the ceremony. It allows you to discuss each of the items with your partner and with your clergy/officiant. It encourages togetherness in planning the wedding ceremony. It helps you personalize your ceremony to convey the importance of this step in your lives and to publicly show the unique quality of your mutual love. The way in which you communicate feelings and ideas, work out differences, and attack common problems during your wedding planning process will provide an indication of how you will handle significant matters in your married life.

WEDDING CEREMONY QUESTIONNAIRE

■ **Date and Time of Ceremony**

Date: _____ 19____

Time: _____ a.m.\p.m.

◆ When selecting the date and time for the service, did you consider religious observances, local customs, and/or seasonal concerns? ☐ Yes ☐ No

■ **Date and Time of Rehearsal**

Date: _____ 19____

Time: _____ a.m./p.m.

■ **Clergy/Officiant**

Name: _____

Title: _____

Address: _____

_____

_____

Telephone: ( )_____

◆ Will you have an assisting clergy/officiant? ☐ Yes ☐ No

Name: _____

Title: _____

Address: _____

_____

_____

Telephone: ( )_____

■ **Bride**

Full Maiden Name: _____

Address: _____

_____

Telephone: (   ) _____ Home

(   ) _____ Work

■ **Groom**

Full Name: _____

Address: _____

_____

Telephone: (   ) _____ Home

(   ) _____ Work

■ **Background Information**

◆ Is this your first marriage?

Bride: ☐ Yes ☐ No If not, number of previous _____

Groom: ☐ Yes ☐ No If not, number of previous _____

◆ Are you renewing your vows? ☐ Yes ☐ No

◆ Are you both of the same faith/denomination?

☐ Yes ☐ No

If not, will the ceremony have clergy from both faiths/denominations? ☐ Yes ☐ No

Note: *Each religion has traditions associated with its wedding service. You can add significance to an interfaith ceremony by learning about the customs of each faith and incorporating something from each into your wedding service.*

■ **Type of Ceremony**

◆ Service: ☐ Traditional ☐ Modified ☐ Contemporary

◆ Style: ☐ Very Formal ☐ Formal ☐ Semiformal

☐ Informal ☐ Nontraditional

◆ Setting: ☐ Church ☐ Club/Hotel ☐ Cruise Ship

☐ Home ☐ Outdoor/Garden ☐ Other

(Specify) _____

■ **Special Ceremonies:**

    ☐ Candlelight ☐ Civil ☐ Clergy

    ☐ Double Wedding ☐ Military ☐ Reaffirmation/ Renewing vows

■ **Size:** ☐ Large (200+ guests)

          ☐ Moderate (100-200 guests)

          ☐ Small (less than 100 guests)

■ **Length:** ☐ 30 minutes or less ☐ More than 30 minutes

■ **Pre-Marital Counseling Sessions**

    ◆ Is pre-marital counseling required? ☐ Yes ☐ No

      If so, how many sessions? _____

      How far in advance of the ceremony must the counseling be completed?

      _____

    ◆ First Session - Date: _____Time: _____a.m./p.m.

      Location: _____

    ◆ Second Session - Date: _____Time: _____a.m./p.m.

      Location: _____

    ◆ Third Session - Date: _____Time: _____a.m./p.m.

      Location: _____

    ◆ Fourth Session - Date: _____Time: _____a.m./p.m.

      Location: _____

    ◆ Fifth Session - Date: _____Time: _____a.m./p.m.

      Location: _____

    ◆ Sixth Session - Date: _____Time: _____a.m./p.m.

      Location: _____

■ Ceremony Site

You may choose almost any site for your wedding ceremony. Your religious beliefs, your desires, your parents' wishes, the degree of tradition, the degree of formality, and the number of guests you expect are the main concerns in selecting a site. Whatever you do should depend on personal taste and the circumstances of your wedding. The site which you ultimately choose, however, should offer the intimacy, ambiance, sentiment, and privacy that you desire as well as sufficient accessibility and practicality.

Important considerations which you should weigh when selecting a wedding site are: your wedding style and theme, physical/aesthetic features, capacity, atmosphere, availability, services offered, and fees.

Preview the sites which you are considering, take photographs (if permitted), and immediately make notes on your reactions/impressions.

Site Name: _____

Site Address: _____

_____

Telephone: (   )_____

* Will the ceremony and reception be held at the same location? ☐ Yes ☐ No

* Does the architecture of the site agree with the style of wedding you want? ☐ Yes ☐ No

* What is the earliest you can arrive? _____ a.m./p.m.

* What is the maximum time allowed for using the site? _____ Hour(s)

* Are there any restrictions or rules imposed by the site? ☐ Yes ☐ No

   If so, what are they? _____

_____

- Will the site comfortably accommodate all of your planned guests? ☐ Yes ☐ No

  What is the site capacity? _____

  How many guests are you expecting? _____

- Does the site have sufficient restroom facilities?

  ☐ Yes ☐ No

- Does the site have access for handicapped guests?

  ☐ Yes ☐ No

- Is there sufficient parking for the wedding party and guests? ☐ Yes ☐ No

  If not, what parking arrangements can be made?

  _____

  _____

- What are the predominant colors?

  Walls _____

  Floors/carpets _____

  Furnishings _____

  Windows _____

  Will any of the colors clash with your color scheme?
  ☐ Yes ☐ No

- Is something available to serve as an altar?

  ☐ Yes ☐ No

  Is there sufficient room at the altar for the clergy/officiant and members of the wedding party? ☐ Yes ☐ No

  Is there sufficient room near the altar for the organist/musicians? ☐ Yes ☐ No

- Does the site provide seating? ☐ Yes ☐ No

  If not, have arrangements been made to have seating brought in? ☐ Yes ☐ No

13

Supplier's Name: _____

Address: _____

_____

Telephone: ( )_____ Date delivered:_____

- Is there an unobstructed view of the ceremony area so that all guests will be able to see? ☐ Yes ☐ No

- What is the lighting like at the time planned for the ceremony?

_____

If during the day, does the sun cause any glares or does it obstruct the views of the clergy/officiant, any of the wedding party, or guests? ☐ Yes ☐ No

- Are there separate dressing rooms for the bride and groom so they may finish getting ready? ☐ Yes ☐ No

If not, have arrangements been made to get ready elsewhere? ☐ Yes ☐ No

Location: (Bride) _____

Telephone: ( )_____

Location: (Groom) _____

Telephone: ( )_____

- Does the site have good acoustics? ☐ Yes ☐ No

Will a public address system be necessary for the clergy/officiant? ☐ Yes ☐ No

If so, is a system provided by the site? ☐ Yes ☐ No

If the site does not provide the system, have arrangements been made to rent a system? ☐ Yes ☐ No

Supplier's Name: _____

Address: _____

_____

Telephone: ( )_____ Date delivered: _____

- Does the site have good ventilation and air conditioning or heating? ☐ Yes ☐ No

  Is the air conditioning or heating system noisy/distracting when operating? ☐ Yes ☐ No

- Have you made reservations? ☐ Yes ☐ No

- If the wedding ceremony is planned for outdoors, has an alternative site been selected in case of bad weather? ☐ Yes ☐ No

  Location: _____

  _____

  _____

  Telephone: (   )_____

■ Additional Considerations

Breaking the Ice

For small- to medium-sized weddings, you may want to have a warm, friendly, cozy atmosphere where you feel close to your guests and want them to feel they are part of the ceremony. However, you may have a situation where many of the guests aren't acquainted with one another, or where the bride's family doesn't know the groom's family.

To remedy this, you may wish to have a pre-ceremony reception where your guests have an opportunity to meet each other. This reception doesn't have to be an elaborate affair. It may be a simple gathering located in close proximity to the ceremony site (i.e. vestibule, lobby, or adajcent room) with punch and coffee. The purpose of the reception is to give the guests a chance to congregate, mingle, and chat before the ceremony. Both the bride and groom may want to designate some family members to arrive early and be available to help with introductions.

As an alternative, you may ask your clergy/officiant to greet your guests after they have been seated, but prior to the seating of the bride's and groom's mothers. At that time, the clergy/officant can introduce himself/herself, explain your desire to have everyone feel comfortable and be a significant part of the ceremony, and ask all the guests to stand and introduce themselves to the people around them.

Children at the Ceremony

You may wish to avoid some of the pitfalls of having young children at your ceremony, such as a baby's cry obliterating your vows. But if many of your family members and friends have children and you don't want to jeopardize their attendance or offend them by excluding the little ones, you may want to consider having a child care area at the ceremony site staffed by either site personnel or teenage family members or friends.

■ **Ceremony Arrangements**

♦ Have you made arrangements to decorate the ceremony site? ☐ Yes ☐ No

What will be the colors of the flowers/decorations?

_____

Who will put up the decorations before the ceremony?

Names: _____

_____

Who will remove the decorations after the ceremony?

Names: _____

_____

♦ Will you use a canopy outside of or over the site, or canopies over both? ☐ Yes ☐ No

If so, who will supply it/them?

☐ Florist ☐ Rental firm ☐ Other

(specify) _____

Supplier's Name: _____

Address:_____

_____

Telephone: (   )_____ Date delivered: _____

◆ Will the guests be seated ? ☐ Yes   ☐ No

   Will the wedding party be seated? ☐ Yes   ☐ No

◆ Will you use candelabras and/or flower stands?

   ☐ Yes   ☐ No

   If so, are they available from the site? ☐ Yes   ☐ No

   If not, who will supply them?

   ☐ Florist ☐ Rental firm ☐ Other

   (specify) _____

   Supplier's Name: _____

   Address:_____

   _____

   Telephone: (   )_____ Date delivered: _____

◆ Will you have a candlelight service? ☐ Yes ☐ No

   Who will supply the candleholders?

   ☐ Florist ☐ Rental firm ☐ Other

   (specify) _____

   Supplier's Name: _____

   Address:_____

   _____

   Telephone: (   ) _____ Date delivered: _____

◆ If permitted by the site, will you use pew candles?

   ☐ Yes ☐ No

17

If so, who will supply the candles?

☐ You ☐ Florist ☐ Rental firm ☐ Other
(specify)_____

Who will light/extinguish the candles?

☐ Ushers ☐ Candle lighters

Names: _____

_____

◆ Will you use pew reservation cards for seating special
guests? ☐ Yes ☐ No

Even if pew reservation cards are not used, how many
seats should be reserved for family and special guests?

_____

◆ Will aisle ribbons be used? ☐ Yes ☐ No

If so, who will arrange them? ☐ Florist ☐ Ushers

☐ Other (specify) _____

If ushers are used, which two ushers will arrange them?

Names: _____

_____

How many rows should be reserved? _____

◆ Will an aisle carpet be used? ☐ Yes ☐ No

If so, who will lay/unroll it? ☐ Florist ☐ Ushers

☐ Other (specify) _____

If ushers are used, which two ushers will lay/unroll
it?

Names: _____

_____

Does the site have any restrictions on how the aisle
carpet can be held down? ☐ Yes ☐ No If so, what
are the restrictions? _____

How long is the aisle? _____ Feet

At what point in the service will it be laid/unrolled?

_____

Who will remove it after the service? ☐ Florist

☐ Ushers ☐ Other (specify) _____

◆ Will you have printed programs? ☐ Yes ☐ No

If so, are they supplied by the site? ☐ Yes ☐ No

If not, have you selected them and arranged to have them printed? ☐ Yes ☐ No

Supplier's Name: _____

Address:_____

_____

Telephone: ( )_____ Date delivered: _____

Printer's Name: _____

Address: _____

_____

Telephone: ( )_____ Date delivered: _____

Note: *A program is especially useful when responsive readings are to be used, and/or when many of the family and friends are from out of the area or of different faiths and are thus not familiar with the procedures.*

◆ Will a guest book be available at the ceremony?

☐ Yes ☐ No

If so, who will supply the table for the guest book?

☐ Site ☐ Rental firm

☐ Other (specify) _____

Who will set up the guest book? _____

Who will transport the guest book to the reception site?

_____

- ◆ Will a gift table be set up at the ceremony site?

  ☐ Yes ☐ No

  If so, who will supply the table? ☐ Site ☐ Rental firm
  ☐ Other (specify) _____

  Who will set up the table? _____

  Who will watch over the gifts during the ceremony and
  move them to the reception site? _____

- ◆ Will there be a processional? ☐ Yes ☐ No

  If so, how will the attendants enter? (See Chapter 9 —
  "How is the Rehearsal Supposed to Go?")

  ☐ Groomsmen and bridesmaids separate, single file

  ☐ Groomsmen and bridesmaids paired together

  ☐ Groomsmen enter single file from side with best man
  and groom

  ☐ Other (please explain) _____

  Which of the following will be used to enter?

  ☐ Center aisle ☐ Side aisle

  ☐ Other (please explain) _____

  _____

- ◆ Do you want an opening prayer? ☐ Yes ☐ No
- ◆ Will the bride be "Given Away"? ☐ Yes ☐ No

  Alternative (Specify) _____

- ◆ Will you choose your Scripture / reading selections?

  ☐ Yes ☐ No

  If so, will the selections be ☐ religious ☐ secular

  ☐ both?

  (See Chapter 13 — "How Can We Personalize Our Ceremony?")

☐ Old Testament Reading

Selection _____ Read By _____

☐ New Testament Reading

Selection _____ Read By _____

☐ Gospel

Selection _____ Read By _____

☐ Other Religious Readings

Selection _____ Read By _____

Selection _____ Read By _____

Selection _____ Read By _____

☐ Secular Reading(s)

Selection _____ Read By _____

Selection _____ Read By _____

Selection _____ Read By _____

Will responsive readings be used? ☐ Yes   ☐ No

Selection _____

Note: *Your selection of readings is an opportunity for you to convey special thoughts about your love and marriage. As a rule of thumb, wedding ceremonies may include three or four readings. They may be religious, secular, or a combination of both. Many churches use at least three: Old Testament, New Testament, and Gospel. When deciding on religious readings, make sure that the translation you are using is acceptable to your clergy/officiant. Your secular selections should also be reviewed by your clergy/officiant to make sure that they are appropriate. (See Chapter 13 — "How Can We Personalize Our Ceremony?")*

♦ Will you use a knee cushion/prayer bench at the altar?
☐ Yes   ☐ No

If so, is it available from the site? ☐ Yes   ☐ No

If it is not available from the site, have you made arrangements to rent one? ☐ Yes ☐ No

Supplier's Name: _____

Address:_____

_____

Telephone: (___)_____ Date delivered: _____

◆ Will you light a unity candle? ☐ Yes ☐ No

If so, who will supply it? ☐ Site ☐ You

◆ Will communion/Eucharist be part of the wedding service? ☐ Yes ☐ No

◆ Will you use any cultural customs (i.e. *lazo* and/or *arras*)? ☐ Yes ☐ No

If yes, specify _____

_____

Note: *It is important to preserve and reflect your ethnic, as well as religious, customs. We need to recognize and appreciate our heritage.*

◆ Do you plan to say anything to each other during the service? ☐ Yes ☐ No

If so, what? _____

_____

_____

◆ Will you write any personal or special vows?

☐ Yes ☐ No

(See Chapter 13 — "How Can We Personalize Our Ceremony?")

If so, are they ☐ replacing, or ☐ in addition to the regular wedding vows?

Do you need pre-approval for the special vows from the clergy/officiant? ☐ Yes ☐ No

+ Do you want the rings blessed as part of the ring exchange? ☐ Yes ☐ No

+ Do you want a marriage prayer/blessing (nuptial blessing)? ☐ Yes ☐ No

+ Do you plan to thank or recognize/acknowledge your parents? ☐ Yes ☐ No

+ If you are planning anything else special or different in your ceremony, please describe it briefly: _____

_____

+ Do you want the clergy/officiant to introduce you as the newly married couple? ☐ Yes ☐ No

+ Do you want the clergy/officiant to make an announcement about the reception? ☐ Yes ☐ No

+ Will there be a recessional? ☐ Yes ☐ No

If so, how will the wedding party leave?

☐ Center aisle ☐ Side aisle

☐ Other (please explain) _____

+ Will you have a receiving line at the wedding site?

☐ Yes ☐ No

+ Does the site permit the throwing of rice or birdseed?

☐ Yes ☐ No

+ Have you made arrangements for custodial services after the ceremony? ☐ Yes ☐ No

Name: _____

Address: _____

_____

Telephone: ( ) _____

23

■ Ceremony Fees/Expenses

- ◆ What are the fees and expenses associated with the use of the site?

Clergy/officiant	$_____
Facility/site	$_____
Organist	$_____
Musicians/soloist	$_____
Custodial	$_____
Supplies	$_____
Aisle runner	$_____
Candles	$_____
Decorations	$_____
Guest book	$_____
Rehearsal	$_____
Other services	$_____
Subtotal Ceremony Fees/ Expenses	$_____

■ Associated Fees/Expenses

Florist	$_____
Photographer	$_____
Videographer	$_____
Parking Attendants	$_____
Drivers	$_____
Rental Cars	$_____
Limousine	$_____
Subtotal Associated Fees/ Expenses	$_____

Subtotal Ceremony Fees/
Expenses $_____

Subtotal Associated Fees/
Expenses $_____

Total Fees/Expenses $_____

CHAPTER 3

Who Will Be in Our Wedding?

There are no hard and fast rules about how many people you should include in your wedding party. The number of attendants you have really depends upon how many you want, the style of the wedding, and the size of the ceremony site.

In making your selection, use some discretion. Give serious thought to those with whom you want to share this experience. You should be certain that the people whom you invite to be your attendants are people whom you want gathered around you on your special day. Try to be considerate by not asking people to be in your wedding who can't afford to buy their attire — unless, of course, you are planning to assist them. Whether the attendants are married or pregnant makes no difference. However, a due date close to the wedding date may make the woman physically uncomfortable and/or self-conscious about her appearance in the bridesmaid dress.

Note: *If either of you have children, asking them to be members of your wedding party is an opportune time to get them actively involved in your wedding ceremony.*

WEDDING PARTY QUESTIONNAIRE

- Maid or Matron of Honor: _____
  Telephone: (   ) _____ Home (   ) _____ Work
- Best Man: _____
  Telephone: (   ) _____ Home (   ) _____ Work
- Person "giving away" bride: _____
  Relation to bride: _____
  Telephone: (   ) _____ Home (   ) _____ Work

Note: *The term "giving away" is currently used to indicate the parents' support and approval of the marriage. Alternatives to asking "Who gives this woman...?" include "Who supports or blesses this marriage?" While it is a rather simple expression, the couple should consider and appreciate its significance. The wedding ceremony is the parents' formal expression of consent to the marriage in the presence of family and friends, and it gives substance to the parental role.*

- Bridesmaids — How many? _____

  _____ Telephone: (   ) _____Home
  (   ) _____ Work

  _____ Telephone: (   ) _____Home
  (   ) _____ Work

  _____ Telephone: (   ) _____Home
  (   ) _____ Work

  _____ Telephone: (   ) _____Home
  (   ) _____ Work

  _____ Telephone: (   ) _____Home
  (   ) _____ Work

  _____ Telephone: (   ) _____Home

( ) _____ Work

_____ Telephone: ( ) _____Home

( ) _____ Work

_____ Telephone: ( ) _____Home

( ) _____ Work

_____ Telephone: ( ) _____Home

( ) _____ Work

_____ Telephone: ( ) _____Home

( ) _____ Work

* Junior Bridesmaids — How many _____

_____ Telephone: ( ) _____Home

_____ Telephone: ( ) _____Home

Note: *These are girls of an "in-between" age — too old to be a flower girl but too young to be a bridesmaid.*

* Ushers / Groomsmen — How many? _____

_____ Telephone: ( ) _____Home

( ) _____ Work

_____ Telephone: ( ) _____Home

( ) _____ Work

_____ Telephone: ( ) _____Home

( ) _____ Work

_____ Telephone: ( ) _____Home

( ) _____ Work

_____ Telephone: ( ) _____Home

( ) _____ Work

_____ Telephone: ( ) _____Home

( ) _____ Work

_____ Telephone: ( ) _____ Home

( ) _____ Work

_____ Telephone: ( ) _____ Home

( ) _____ Work

_____ Telephone: ( ) _____ Home

( ) _____ Work

_____ Telephone: ( ) _____ Home

( ) _____ Work

- Who will be assigned as head usher? _____

Note: *The size of the wedding determines the number of ushers. There is usually a minimum of one usher per 25 to 50 guests. It is the groom's decision to designate the number of ushers and who his attendants are. The groomsmen may double as ushers if you are trying to keep the size of your wedding party down. It is not necessary to have the same number of groomsmen as bridesmaids, but the wedding party has a better balance when the number is equal.*

- Junior Groomsmen — How many? _____

_____ Telephone: ( ) _____ Home

_____ Telephone: ( ) _____ Home

Note: *These are boys who are too old to be ring bearers or train bearers, but too young to be ushers/groomsmen. If they are old enough, they may be asked to light the candles, attach the aisle ribbons, and/or lay the aisle carpet.*

- Flower Girls — How many? _____

_____

Age: _____ Telephone: ( )_____Home

_____

Age: _____ Telephone: ( )_____Home

+ Ring Bearer:

_____

Age: _____ Telephone: (   )_____Home
+ Pages — How many? _____

_____

Age: _____ Telephone: (   )_____Home

_____

Age: _____ Telephone: (   )_____Home
+ Organist
_____ Telephone: (   ) _____Home
(   ) _____ Work

+ Soloist
_____ Telephone: (   ) _____Home
(   ) _____ Work

+ Other Musicians
_____ Telephone: (   ) _____Home
(   ) _____ Work

_____ Telephone: (   ) _____Home
(   ) _____ Work

+ Wedding Consultant / Advisor
_____ Telephone: (   ) _____Home
Telephone: (   ) _____ Work

+ Is there anyone in the wedding party who has a physical problem that requires special consideration?

☐ Yes ☐ No

If yes, what is the nature of the problem?

_____

■ **Apparel**

◆ What will be the color and style of the bridesmaids' apparel?

_____

◆ Dresses

Bridal shop: _____

Address: _____

_____

Telephone: (   ) _____Hours: _____

Contact: _____

Fitting date: _____Pickup date: _____

◆ Headpiece

Shop: _____

Address: _____

_____

Telephone: (   ) _____Hours: _____

Contact: _____

Fitting date: _____Pickup date: _____

◆ Shoes

Shop: _____

Address: _____

_____

Telephone: (   ) _____Hours: _____

Contact: _____

Fitting date: _____Pickup date: _____

◆ What will be the color and style of the groomsmen's apparel?

_____

◆ Formal Wear:

Shop: _____

Address: _____

_____

Telephone: ( ) _____Hours: _____

Contact: _____

Fitting date: _____ Pickup date: _____

Deposit: _____ Return date: _____

Package includes: _____

_____

Note: *The style of the wedding service impacts the wedding party attire/clothes. The wedding party clothes follow a traditional pattern. Also, proper dress varies with the hour and the season (See Chapter 11).*

◆ Have arrangements been made for the flower girl's basket and the ring bearer's pillow? ☐ Yes ☐ No

◆ Where will the wedding party dress?

Bride: ☐ Home ☐ Site

Maid of Honor: ☐ Home ☐ Bride's home ☐ Site

Bridesmaids: ☐ Home ☐ Bride's home ☐ Site

Groom: ☐ Home ☐ Groom's home ☐ Site

Best Man: ☐ Home ☐ Groom's home ☐ Site

Ushers: ☐ Home ☐ Groom's home ☐ Site

CHAPTER 4

What Music Do We Want?

Do not take the music for granted. Even though you will probably be too excited and nervous to notice what is playing, music is an important aspect of your ceremony. It sets the tone of, and adds meaning to, the service. Therefore, choose the music and where it is performed carefully. Use it to create both a solemn and joyous mood. But remember that too much music can detract from the service. You should contact the site and the ceremony clergy/officiant to determine whether there are any restrictions on the type of music that can be used.

There is so much beautiful music appropriate for weddings that you may find it helpful to listen to some pieces before making your selections. And, should someone suggest a piece of music, make sure that you are familiar with it before using it. If your selection is unusual or out of the ordinary, make sure the musicians have sufficient time to practice it.

Protestant ceremonies usually can include both popular and religious music.

Some Roman Catholic priests limit the music to religious selections and hymns and do not allow popular music.

Conservative and Reform Jewish rabbis may permit the use of popular music, while Orthodox rabbis normally restrict the music to traditional Hebrew compositions. It is customary to have a cantor chant the benedictions ordinarily read by the officiant.

WEDDING MUSIC QUESTIONNAIRE

◆ What music will be used (titles) and when?

☐ Prelude

_____	_____
_____	_____
_____	_____

Note: _If music is used as a prelude, it should start approximately half an hour before the service._

☐ Soloist/choir/ensemble prior to processional

_____

Note: _Vocal music is often used in wedding ceremonies. In some churches, it is traditional to have a soloist, choir, or small ensemble perform immediately after the bride's mother has been seated and prior to the service._

☐ Processional

_____

Note: _The "Bridal Chorus" from Lohengrin is the most frequently used music for the processional, followed by Mendelssohn's "Wedding March" from "A Midsummer Night's Dream." Whatever music you select, just make sure that it has a rhythm and timing conducive for walking down the aisle._

☐ Bride's entrance

_____

☐ Background during service

_____	_____
_____	_____
_____	_____

☐ Soloists/choir/ensemble during service

At what point:_____ Selection: _____

_____   _____

_____   _____

☐ Recessional

_____

☐ Postlude

_____   _____

_____   _____

_____   _____

• Do the site organist/musicians have to be used?

☐ Yes ☐ No

In either case, have arrangements for organist/musicians been made? ☐ Yes ☐ No

What are the arrangements? _____

Note: *For a church wedding, you may allow the church organist to select or suggest appropriate music for the prelude and postlude since he or she is familiar with the church's wedding procedures and has a wide variety of selections from which to choose.*

• Will a soloist/professional musicians be used?

☐ Yes ☐ No

If so, Name: _____

Address: _____

_____

Telephone: (   )_____

Manager's name: _____

Telephone: (   )_____

Union: _____

Date and time of audition: _____

_____a.m./p.m.

37

Price: $_____

- What will be the musicians' attire? _____

- Can recorded music be used? ☐ Yes ☐ No

  If so, does the site have good quality audio equipment? ☐ Yes ☐ No

  If not, will there be sufficient time to set up audio equipment before the ceremony and to remove it afterwards? ☐ Yes ☐ No

- Will you be using recorded music? ☐ Yes ☐ No

  If so, who will be responsible for taping and labeling the music? _____

- Who will operate the audio equipment? _____

- Does the site have the necessary electrical/equipment connections? ☐ Yes ☐ No

CHAPTER 5

ᏔᏏhat About Flowers?

Flowers play an important role in enhancing your wedding style. They bring beauty, color, and elegance to the setting while underscoring a wealth of tradition. Every flower expresses a sentiment; an ambiance you want to create. Flowers symbolize the marriage growing in love and devotion.

FLORIST QUESTIONNAIRE

◆ Will a florist be used? ☐ Yes ☐ No

   If so, Name: _____

            Address: _____

                    _____

            Telephone: (   ) _____

◆ Does the florist specialize in wedding ceremonies?

   ☐ Yes ☐ No

◆ What is the color scheme for your flowers? _____

◆ What varieties of flowers/arrangements will be used?

   _____

◆ What type of flowers/arrangements will be used?

   ☐ Real ☐ Artificial ☐ Combination

◆ Will the bride carry a flower-covered Bible or prayer book instead of a bouquet? ☐ Yes ☐ No

◆ What bouquets/corsages will the florist provide?

   ☐ Bride ☐ Toss-away for reception ☐ Honor attendant ☐ Bridesmaids/junior bridesmaids ☐ Bride's and groom's mothers ☐ Bride's and groom's grandmothers ☐ Special guests

Note: *The bridesmaids' bouquets should be identical. However, the honor attendant's bouquet may be varied to set her apart. The mothers'/grandmothers' corsages do not need to be identical but should be coordinated with the color of their dresses.*

◆ What boutonnieres will the florist provide?

☐ Groom ☐ Groomsmen/ushers/junior ushers ☐ Bride's and groom's fathers ☐ Bride's and groom's grandfathers ☐ Ring bearer ☐ Pages/train bearer

◆ Is your florist familiar with the site you have selected? ☐ Yes ☐ No

If not, when will the florist visit the site? _____

◆ Where will flowers/arrangements be placed?

☐ Altar ☐ Stands ☐ Candelabra ☐ Canopy ☐ Pews/ aisle posts ☐ Window sills ☐ Kneel cushion/prayer bench

◆ Have you obtained written estimates? ☐ Yes ☐ No

If so, what is the price? $_____

◆ Is a deposit required? ☐ Yes ☐ No

If so, how much? $_____

◆ How far in advance must the order be placed _____

◆ What is the cancellation policy? _____

◆ If the wedding party is dressing at a different site(s) from the ceremony, have arrangements been made get the bouquets/corsages and boutonnieres to the dressing site(s)? ☐ Yes ☐ No

What are the arrangements? _____

◆ How early can the florist be at the site to set up the flowers?_____a.m./p.m. _____ minutes before ceremony

◆ Who will transport the flowers from the ceremony site to the reception site? _____

Note: *Some Roman Catholic churches feel that flowers that are part of the wedding take on the spirit of the sacrament and should remain in the church for others to share.*

CHAPTER 6

Who Should We Get to Take Photos and Video?

While your wedding ceremony will be over in a matter of minutes, your pictures and/or videotape will be a lasting reminder of your special day. The photographs and/or videotapes create a pictorial remembrance of the wedding. Through them, you will be able to relive those precious memories with family and friends.

Today many couples are hiring both a photographer and videographer. The videographer collects wedding memories that extend beyond the traditional photographs. Videotape records not only images, but voices, music, movement, and spontaneous moments. With its movie-like qualities, a videotape can capture a wink at the altar as well as friends and relatives offering congratulations.

But a videotape, no matter how well done, is not a substitute for the wedding day portraits that only a photographer can provide. The two media are complementary.

No matter which media you choose, the person must be discreet — never detracting from the ceremony and being sensitive to the mood of you and your families. It is important that the person have experience recording weddings. They should be knowledgeable of wedding etiquette and protocol.

PHOTOGRAPHER/VIDEOGRAPHER QUESTIONNAIRE

- Will a professional photographer and/or videographer be used? ☐ Yes ☐ No

  If so, has one been selected? ☐ Yes ☐ No

- Does the photographer/videographer specialize in wedding ceremonies?

  Photographer: ☐ Yes ☐ No

  Videographer: ☐ Yes ☐ No

- Have you checked their references and/or seen them in action at a wedding? ☐ Yes ☐ No

- Has time been scheduled both before and after the ceremony for photographs? ☐ Yes ☐ No

- Are there any special pictures that you want taken at the wedding site either before, during, and/or after the service? ☐ Yes ☐ No

  If so, what?_____

  _____

  _____

- Have you discussed your picture-taking plans with the site officials and/or your clergy/officiant?

  ☐ Yes ☐ No

- Are there any restrictions on photographer/videographer activities at the ceremony site? ☐ Yes ☐ No

  If so, what?_____

  _____

  _____

■ **Candid Photographs**

If you are trying to economize on the cost of a professional photographer or would like to supplement the number

46

of candid photographs you have taken, some of the camera manufacturers offer disposable cameras in decorated wedding packs. The idea is that you encourage your guests to take photographs by distributing the disposable cameras prior to the ceremony. At the end of your special day, the person whom you designate collects the cameras, or you provide a labeled collection basket where guests may return the cameras in order to get the photographs developed.

■ **Photographer**

    Name: _____

    Address: _____

    _____

    Telephone: (   ) _____

   ◆ What does your wedding package include?

    _____ _____

    _____ _____

    _____ _____

   ◆ What is the price? $_____

   ◆ Is a deposit required? ☐ Yes ☐ No

    If so, how much? $_____

   ◆ How many hours does the package include?_____

   ◆ How is overtime handled?_____

   ◆ How far in advance must reservations be made? _____

   ◆ What is the cancellation policy? _____

   ◆ Have you seen samples of the photographer's work?
    ☐ Yes ☐ No

   ◆ Were the prints in focus? ☐ Yes ☐ No

   ◆ Did the colors seem natural? ☐ Yes ☐ No

   ◆ How creative was the work? _____

Did the photographs show emotions? ☐ Yes ☐ No

◆ Are any special effects available? ☐ Yes ☐ No

If so, what?_____

_____

_____

◆ Have you talked with the photographer you've chosen to shoot your wedding? ☐ Yes ☐ No

If so, who? _____

Do you feel comfortable with the person? ☐ Yes ☐ No

◆ What kind of camera equipment will the person use?

_____

◆ What is the format? ☐ 35mm ☐ 120mm

☐ Other _____

◆ Are the prints hand (custom)- or machine-printed?

☐ Hand (custom) ☐ Machine

◆ What is the cost for reprints?

Size _____ $ _____ Size _____ $ _____

Size _____ $ _____ Size _____ $ _____

Size _____ $ _____ Size _____ $ _____

◆ Is the photographer familiar with the site you have selected? ☐ Yes ☐ No

◆ What will the photographer's attire be?_____

◆ Are the negatives available? ☐ Yes ☐ No

If so, are they an additional cost? ☐ Yes ☐ No

Cost? $ _____

How long are the negatives kept? _____

◆ How soon after the wedding will the proofs be ready?

_____

■ **Videographer**

Name: _____

Address: _____

_____

Telephone: ( ) _____

+ What is the price? $_____
+ Is a deposit required? ☐ Yes ☐ No
  If so, how much? $_____
+ How many hours does the price include? _____
+ How is overtime handled? _____
+ How far in advance must reservations be made? _____
+ What is the cancellation policy? _____
+ Have you seen a sample of the videographer's work?
  ☐ Yes ☐ No
+ Is there movement in the tape? ☐ Yes ☐ No
+ Does the tape seem to jump around? ☐ Yes ☐ No
+ Does it tell a story? ☐ Yes ☐ No
+ Can interviews be interspersed throughout the tape?
  ☐ Yes ☐ No
+ Can it be serious or humorous? ☐ Yes ☐ No
+ What does the package include?
  Unedited tape ☐ Yes ☐ No
  Multi-camera ☐ Yes ☐ No
  Montage of stills ☐ Yes ☐ No
  Titles ☐ Yes ☐ No
  Narration ☐ Yes ☐ No
  Background music ☐ Yes ☐ No

49

Close-up shots ☐ Yes ☐ No

Interviews with family, wedding party, and guests
☐ Yes ☐ No

Other (specify) _____

* Are creative options available? ☐ Yes ☐ No
  If so, what?

  _____   _____

  _____   _____

  _____   _____

* Are you given the opportunity to select the background music? ☐ Yes ☐ No

  Is there a large selection of background music to choose from? ☐ Yes ☐ No

* Is broadcast-quality editing equipment used?
  ☐ Yes ☐ No

* Does the person use consumer or commercial quality camera equipment? _____

* What kind of camera equipment will be used?

  _____

* What is the format? ☐ ¾" ☐ 1" ☐ Other _____

* Will there be sufficient light available at the time and location of the ceremony to videotape? ☐ Yes ☐ No

* Does the videographer maintain the tape? ☐ Yes ☐ No
  If so, for how long? _____

* What is the cost for additional tapes? $_____

* Is the videographer familiar with the site you have selected? ☐ Yes ☐ No

* What will the videographer's attire be? _____

CHAPTER 7

How Should We Handle Parking?

It is not required that you provide parking attendants. However, depending upon the size, style, and location of the ceremony, you may want to have parking attendants park guests' cars. This is particularly true if there is no convenient parking in the vicinity of the ceremony site.

In many instances, members of the wedding party and guests will arrive at the site randomly. However, at the completion of the ceremony, large groups of people may be leaving at the same time for the reception. Therefore, you may find that the site and/or local law enforcement may require that you provide traffic control.

PARKING ARRANGEMENTS QUESTIONNAIRE

* Do you plan on using professional parking attendants at the ceremony site? ☐ Yes ☐ No

  Name: _____

  Address: _____

  _____

  Telephone: (   ) _____

* What is the price? $ _____

* Is a deposit required? ☐ Yes ☐ No

  If so, how much? $ _____

* How many hours does the package include? _____

* How is overtime handled? _____

* How far in advance must reservations be made? _____

* What is the cancellation policy? _____

* What will the attendant(s) wear? _____

* At what time will the attendant(s) arrive?

  _____ a.m./p.m.

* At what time will the attendant(s) leave?

  _____ a.m./p.m.

* Does the attendant(s) have a valid driver's license?

  ☐ Yes ☐ No

* Does the company have appropriate insurance?

  ☐ Yes ☐ No

* What is the cancellation policy? _____

◆ What services are included?

    _____   _____

    _____   _____

    _____   _____

◆ Will the police or sheriff's department require special traffic control? ☐ Yes ☐ No

If so, have arrangements been made? ☐ Yes ☐ No

What are the arrangements? _____

_____

_____

CHAPTER 8

How Will We Get To and From the Ceremony?

Carefully planning the transportation for you, your wedding party, and out-of-town guests will help make your wedding day run smoothly.

Send out-of-town guests an itinerary of your schedule so that they can arrive in time for the wedding, the reception and any other special events.

Relatives and friends who will provide transportation should be given written instructions detailing who they will be transporting, where they are to be, and when they must arrive at each location. They should also be provided with money for gasoline and a car wash.

It may be advantageous to make arrangements with a local hotel/motel to provide the accommodations for all of your out-of-town guests. Normally, the establishments will be willing to give you special rates, will pick up your guests at the airport and, in some instances, will allow the use of their limousine service to take your guests to the ceremony.

TRANSPORTATION QUESTIONNAIRE

■ **Before the Ceremony**

- Will out-of-town guests be using their own vehicles?

  ☐ Yes ☐ No

  If not, will relatives and/or friends be available for transportation? ☐ Yes ☐ No

- What relative/friend will be assigned to what out-of-town guest?

  Driver 1: _____ Telephone: ( )_____

  Guest: _____ Telephone: ( )_____

  Pickup Location: _____

  Pickup Time: _____ a.m./p.m.

  Directions: _____

  Driver 2: _____ Telephone: ( )_____

  Guest: _____ Telephone: ( )_____

  Pickup Location: _____

  Pickup Time: _____ a.m./p.m.

  Directions: _____

  Driver 3: _____ Telephone: ( )_____

  Guest: _____ Telephone: ( )_____

  Pickup Location: _____

  Pickup Time: _____ a.m./p.m.

  Directions: _____

  Driver 4: _____ Telephone: ( )_____

  Guest: _____ Telephone: ( )_____

  Pickup Location: _____

  Pickup Time: _____ a.m./p.m.

  Directions: _____

Driver 5: _____ Telephone: ( )_____

Guest: _____ Telephone: ( )_____

Pickup Location: _____

Pickup Time: _____ a.m./p.m.

Directions: _____

- Has the driver(s) been notified whom to transport, from where, and when? ☐ Yes ☐ No
- Will rental vehicles be used? ☐ Yes ☐ No

  If yes, how many? _____
- For what time period?_____ a.m./p.m. to _____ a.m./p.m.
- When and where will the rental vehicles be picked up?

  _____ a.m./p.m.

  Name: _____

  Address: _____

  _____

  Telephone: ( ) _____
- What is the rental fee? $_____
- When and where will the rental vehicles be returned?

  _____ a.m./p.m.

  Name: _____

  Address: _____

  _____

  Telephone: ( ) _____
- What arrangements have been made for transporting the bride, her parents, and attendants to the ceremony?

  ☐ Private vehicles — Who will drive?

  _____

_____

_____

☐ Rental vehicles — Who will drive?

_____

_____

_____

☐ Chauffeur-driven limousine

☐ Other (e.g. horse-drawn carriage or bridal van)

If so, specify _____

Note: *When more than one vehicle is used to transport the bride, her parents and attendants to the ceremony, the following procession order is used:*

Vehicle 1 — Bride's mother, maid/matron of honor, and possibly an attendant

Vehicle 2 — Attendants

Vehicle 3 — Bride and her father

◆ When and where will the rental vehicles be picked up?

_____ a.m./p.m.

Name: _____

Address: _____

_____

Telephone: (   ) _____

◆ When and where will the rental vehicles be returned?

_____ a.m./p.m.

Name: _____

Address: _____

_____

Telephone: (   ) _____

+ What arrangements have been made for transporting the groom, his best man, and groomsmen to the ceremony? (Optional)

Note: *The groom, best man, and groomsmen normally make their own arrangements for getting to the ceremony.*

☐ Private vehicles — Who will drive? _____

☐ Rental vehicles — Who will drive? _____

☐ Chauffeur-driven limousine

☐ Other (e.g. horse-drawn carriage or bridal van)

If so, specify _____

+ If limousines or other vehicles are used, what is the price? $_____

Name: _____

Address: _____

_____

Telephone: (   ) _____

What is the minimum rental period? _____

How many passengers will it hold? _____

How is overtime handled? _____

What is the cancellation policy? _____

What services are included?

_____   _____

_____   _____

_____   _____

+ Is a deposit required? ☐ Yes ☐ No
  If so, how much? $_____

+ What is the policy on decorating the vehicles?
  ☐ Permitted ☐ Not Permitted

- Are the vehicles available for inspection prior to rental? ☐ Yes ☐ No

  If so, where and when _____ a.m./p.m.

- How far in advance must reservations be made?

  _____

- What is the insurance coverage?_____

- What will the chauffeur/driver wear? _____

■ **Transportation Assignments**

- Bride and her father/escort

  Location: _____

  Pickup time: _____ a.m./p.m. Driver: _____

- Maid of Honor and the bride's mother

  Name: _____

  Location: _____

  Pickup time: _____ a.m./p.m. Driver: _____

- Bridesmaids

  1. Name: _____

  Location: _____

  Pickup time: _____ a.m./p.m. Driver: _____

  2. Name: _____

  Location: _____

  Pickup time: _____ a.m./p.m. Driver: _____

  3. Name: _____

  Location: _____

  Pickup time: _____ a.m./p.m. Driver: _____

  4. Name: _____

  Location: _____

  Pickup time: _____ a.m./p.m. Driver: _____

5. Name: _____

Location: _____

Pickup time: _____ a.m./p.m. Driver: _____

6. Name: _____

Location: _____

Pickup time: _____ a.m./p.m. Driver: _____

7. Name: _____

Location: _____

Pickup time: _____ a.m./p.m. Driver: _____

8. Name: _____

Location: _____

Pickup time: _____ a.m./p.m. Driver: _____

■ **After the Ceremony**

 ◆ What arrangements have been made for leaving the ceremony?

☐ Private vehicles — Who will drive?

_____

_____

_____

☐ Rental vehicles — Who will drive?

_____

_____

_____

☐ Chauffeur-driven limousine

☐ Other (e.g. horse-drawn carriage)

If so, specify _____

Note: *The bride and groom should ride in the same vehicle that brought the bride and her father to the ceremony. The bride's parents should be in another vehicle, and the rest of the wedding party in the remaining vehicles. If other arrangements have not been made, the groomsmen or ushers transport the bridesmaids to the reception.*

CHAPTER 9

ℋow Is the Rehearsal Supposed to Go?

In all but the small, simple, informal ceremony, you should plan to have a rehearsal a day or two before the actual ceremony. A rehearsal for a ceremony of any size is reassuring; however, as tensions build toward the wedding day, the rehearsal can also be one of the most nervous times.

The wedding rehearsal is the time for you, the wedding party, and other ceremony participants to:

- Practice and become familiar with the entire ceremony.

- Go over any special variations requested.

- Pick up the "cues" for responses.

- Make arrangements for unexpected situations.

You should make arrangements with your clergy/officiant well in advance to schedule the rehearsal at the wedding site.

While your ideas for the ceremony should have been discussed with your clergy/officiant during a pre-wedding conference, the rehearsal is the time to make specific choices and decisions about the conduct of the service. In order to ensure that the service runs smoothly and to work out all the last-minute details, the clergy/officiant, all members of the wedding party, the organist, musicians, and the soloist should be present. The former practice of having the maid of honor stand in for the bride is not normally followed today.

Things to remember about the rehearsal are:

- The rehearsal should take at least an hour. Encourage the wedding party to arrive on time.

- Your clergy / officiant is in charge.

- The wedding party should pay attention to the instructions and respond quickly.

- If you disagree with what is being done, discuss your opinions openly.

While your clergy / officiant is in charge, you should plan enough time to go over the procedures two or three times to make sure that everyone knows what to do. This is the time to make sure that everyone does a "run through" of his or her part. The first time, your clergy / officiant should go through the ceremony step by step, explaining what everyone is supposed to do. Then the entire ceremony should be practiced at least once more. The second time the participants should be more relaxed and should be better able to remember what they are supposed to do.

Either before or after the rehearsal, the clergy / officiant may wish to brief the ushers on their duties and have them walk through their various responsibilities. If time permits, the clergy / officiant may wish to practice all their responsibilities as well. This can includes lighting the candles, seating the guests and family, unrolling the aisle runner, assembling for the processional, and returning to excuse the guests after the recessional.

To start out, your clergy / officiant may ask you to come forward and take your places in front of him or her, facing the altar. Then the best man will be asked to take his position at the groom's right and maid or matron of honor to take her position at the bride's left. Once in place, you may be asked to arrange your attendants as you prefer. Your clergy / officiant will help you arrange your party in the most advantageous manner that the space and design of the site permits.

It is a good idea to bring along "dummy" bouquets to use as you practice passing your flowers. If your wedding dress has a train, it is also a good idea to bring a tablecloth or some other material to simulate your train so that you can practice maneuvering with the train and your maid/matron of honor can practice adjusting it.

If the ceremony site has a raised area at the altar, you may be asked whether you want part of the ceremony performed on the raised area or whether you want the entire ceremony performed on the floor level. If you elect to use the raised area, you will need to decide what members of the wedding party you want to accompany you.

Your clergy/officiant may wish to listen to any special music you have selected. If you are planning to memorize your vows, the rehearsal is also a good time to give your clergy/officiant a copy in case you forget your lines during the ceremony.

In some instances neither the clergy/officiant nor the site is available for a rehearsal. In that case, everyone in the wedding party should assemble at the site early on the day of the ceremony to receive instructions before the ceremony begins.

Note: *The person escorting the bride and giving her away or blessing the marriage does not have to be a male. It could be the bride's mother or a close female relative. Likewise, the honor attendant does not have to be female, and the person standing up with the groom does not have to be male.*

If someone takes the place of the bride's father, that person then joins the bride's mother in the first row. If the father is a widower and the bride has asked a female relative to take the mother's place, she sits in the front row with the father.

While members of the wedding party are not required to be of the same faith as the bride and groom, they are expected to take part in all of the observed customs. If anyone feels uncomfortable about this, he/she should decline when first asked to be part of the wedding party.

❑ Processional (See Figure 9-1, pages 77-82)

Your clergy/officiant will explain the following items associated with the processional, help you decide on your preferences, and arrange your party in the most advantageous manner within the space and design of the site:

- ◆ What will the order of the wedding party be for the processional?

- ◆ What kind of step will be used for the processional?

- ◆ What happens if the site does not have a center aisle?

■ Protestant

After the bride's mother is seated, two ushers may attach the aisle ribbons and unroll the aisle carpet. As the music begins, the clergy, followed by the groom and best man, make their way to the altar from the side of the chancel. Groomsmen enter in pairs from the narthex (rear), lined up according to your arrangement. At the chancel rail or first row, the groomsmen take their places on the right side with the groom and best man, half facing the guests, watching the approach of the bride and her father. The groomsmen are followed by the junior groomsmen, if any.

Next come the bridesmaids who walk individually unless there are more than four. If there is an odd number, the shortest bridesmaid walks alone before the pairs. At the chancel rail or front row, the bridesmaids take their places on the left side, half facing the guests, watching the approach of the bride and her father/escort. The bridesmaids are followed by the junior bridesmaids, if any. Next in order is the honor attendant followed by the ring bearer and flower girl.

The bride's mother gives the cue to stand when the bride, holding her father's/escort's right or left arm (depending on the clergy's instructions), enters with pages, if any, carrying the train behind her dress.

A short, natural step is recommended, with no hesitation or sliding of the foot, and maintaining an equal distance of about six to eight feet between members of the wedding party as they walk down the nave (center aisle). The exception in the spacing is the bride and her father/escort. They should be approximately twelve feet behind the flower girl. The step should be in perfect rhythm, with the music and the organist providing the proper tempo.

If the site has two side aisles rather than one center aisle, the procession uses the left aisle (from the narthex, facing the altar) and the recession uses the right aisle.

Variations

1) The groomsmen enter in the procession individually in the order of your arrangement.

2) The groomsmen and the bridesmaids walk side by side, bridesmaid on the left, separating at the front row as they approach the altar.

3) The groom, the best man, and the groomsmen enter the altar area from the side following the clergy/officiant and turn slightly toward the rear before the bridesmaids start down the aisle to watch the bride's arrival.

- **Catholic** (Roman)

If there is no procession, the priest either greets the bride and groom at the church vestibule door or at the altar for the rite of welcome.

If the rite of welcome is to be omitted, the wedding ceremony immediately begins with the Mass.

If there is a procession, the couple may observe the same processional procedure described above, but the priest meets and greets the couple at the church vestibule door and leads them and their attendants to the altar.

- **Jewish**

The groomsmen enter individually or in pairs from the rear, followed by the best man, and the groom with both his parents. The bridesmaids enter singly or in pairs, followed by the honor attendant, the flower girl, and the ring bearer, and the bride and her parents.

If the site does not have a center aisle, the wedding party should enter by the left aisle and leave by the right aisle.

Variations

The procession is led by the rabbi and cantor, followed by the bride's grandparents, the groom's grandparents, the groomsmen, the best man, the groom with his parents, the bridesmaids, the honor attendant, the ring bearer, the flower girl, and the bride with her parents.

◻ At the Altar (See Figure 9-2, pages 83-86)

As with the processional, your clergy/officiant will offer recommendations on the following items, help you decide on your preferences, and arrange your party in the most advantageous manner within the space and design of the site:

- How will the wedding party be arranged at the altar?

- How will the groomsmen hold their hands?

- Will the wedding party stand or sit?

- Will the children in the wedding party stand or sit?

- Will you face the altar, the guests, or a combination of both?

- Where will the soloist/musicians be located?

- Will a platform (raised altar area) be used, if available and practical? If so, what members of the wedding party will accompany you? At what point in the ceremony will you and your party move to the platform?

- Who will turn the bride's veil back and when?

- How will the bride pass her bouquet to her maid of honor? If the wedding is to be a double ring ceremony, will both the bride's and the honor attendant's bouquets be passed to bridesmaids?

• How will the ring exchange take place? Is the ring bearer old enough to carry the real rings attached to his pillow? What happens if a ring is dropped?

• What happens if someone becomes ill or faints?

Note: *In most cases, your clergy/officiant will prompt your responses and movements during the actual ceremony if you forget anything.*

■ Protestant

The groomsmen form a diagonal line to the right behind the groom and best man. The bridesmaids form a similar line to the left side behind the bride and honor attentant. The ring bearer stands near the best man. The flower girl stands near the honor attendant. The bride leaves her father's/escort's arm as she reaches the chancel rail or first aisle and is passed to the groom. The groom moves toward the bride on her right side, and she accepts his arm. The best man and honor attendant take their places alongside the groom and bride. The bride's father/escort remains standing behind her and a little to the left until the clergy/officiant asks, "Who gives this woman to be married...?" or "Who supports and blesses this marriage?" at which time the father/escort responds and sits down in the first row on the left side beside the bride's mother.

The bride passes her bouquet to the honor attendant prior to the exchanging of vows. The best man and honor attendant participate in the ring ceremony. If the bride and groom are required to go up steps or to kneel at the altar, the groom assists the bride. The groom or honor attendant lifts the bride's veil for the kiss, which is a tradition to ensure that the groom is the first person to kiss his wife. The honor attendant passes the bride's bouquet back to her. The honor attendant or pages then arrange the bride's train as the bride turns toward the guests for the recessional. The clergy/officiant then introduces the new couple.

Variations

1) The groomsmen and bridesmaids stand in pairs on each side with each bridesmaid even with or one step in front of each usher.

2) A contemporary variation is for the bridesmaids and groomsmen to form a semicircle around the bride and groom.

■ **Catholic** (Roman)

Sometimes the bride is not given away. Therefore, the bride's father places the bride's hand in the groom's, turns away once the bride reaches the altar and joins the bride's mother. The father may lift his daughter's veil and kiss her before joining his wife.

■ **Jewish**

The ceremony is performed under a chuppah (covering) held up by some friends or relatives. The bride's and groom's parents remain standing throughout the ceremony.

❑ **Recessional** (See Figure 9-3, pages 87-90)

Your clergy/officiant will discuss the following items associated with the recessional and help you decide on your preferences:

* What is the order of the recessional?

* What happens if the site does not have a center aisle?

The recessional begins when the organist/musicians sound the recessional march, which is slightly faster. The order of the recessional is the reverse of the processional. The bride takes the groom's right arm and starts up the aisle, followed by the pages or train bearers. The flower girl and ring bearer pair off, followed by the honor attendant and best man, the bridesmaids on the right arm of the groomsmen. If the ring bearer has imitation rings tied or sewn to pillow, he turns the pillow over so they do not show during the recessional.

The ushers escort out the mothers and honored guests. If aisle ribbons are used, two ushers remove the ribbons a row at a time from front to back, signaling the guests to file out. The wedding party forms a receiving line in the vestibule or front of the site (optional). The bride, groom, and their witnesses (honor attendant and best man) meet with the clergy/officiant to sign the marriage license and certificates unless the signing is incorporated into the ceremony. The wedding party returns to the site to pose for photographs.

Normally there is no recessional in a home or club/hotel wedding. The couple turns to receive the congratulations of both sets of parents. The receiving line is then formed and other guests come to greet the newlyweds.

Variations

1) If the bridesmaids outnumber the groomsmen, one groomsman may escort two bridesmaids. If the groomsmen outnumber the bridesmaids, the extra groomsmen can walk together at the end of the procession.

2) The attendants precede the newlyweds, who stop at each row and greet guests as they exit.

☐ Receiving Line (See Figure 9-4, page 91)

If you are planning on having a receiving line at the wedding site immediately after the ceremony, you may want to practice the formation. The configuration of the receiving line is driven by the assumption that the bride's mother is the host and has responsibility for presenting/introducing guests to the groom's parents. Therefore, the first person in the receiving line is the bride's mother, followed in order by: the bride's father, the groom's mother, the groom's father, the bride and groom, the honor attendant, and the bridesmaids. It is optional for the bride's and groom's fathers to take part in the receiving line. The best man and groomsmen do not participate in the receiving line. If the bride's parents are divorced, it is usually the bride's mother who heads the receiving line.

75

Variations

1) The bride's mother, the groom's mother, the bride and groom, the honor attendant, and the bridesmaids.

2) The bride's mother, the groom's father, the groom's mother, the bride's father, the bride and groom, the honor attendant, and the bridesmaids.

❒ Other

- ◆ Provide ushers with instructions of their duties.

- ◆ Provide any special seating arrangements to the head usher.

- ◆ What happens if a bridesmaid or groomsman has to drop out at the last minute?

- ◆ What happens if an uninvited guest shows up?

Figure 9-1, Processional Formations
Christian Ceremony

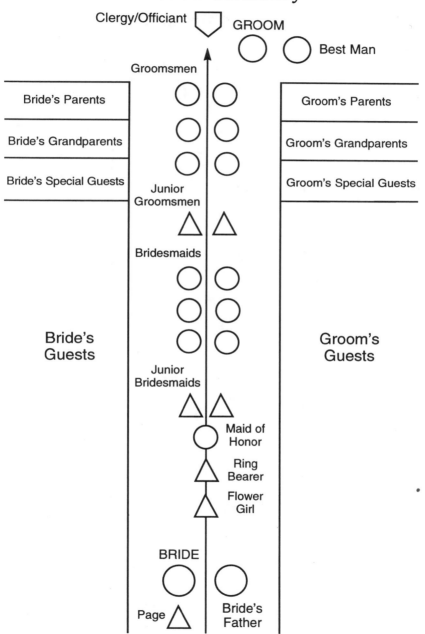

Clergy/Officiant

GROOM

Best Man

Groomsmen

Bride's Parents

Groom's Parents

Bride's Grandparents

Groom's Grandparents

Bride's Special Guests

Groom's Special Guests

Junior
Groomsmen

Bridesmaids

Bride's
Guests

Groom's
Guests

Junior
Bridesmaids

Maid of
Honor

Ring
Bearer

Flower
Girl

BRIDE

Page

Bride's
Father

Figure 9-1, Processional Formations
Christian Ceremony - Variation 1

Clergy/Officiant

GROOM

Best Man

Groomsmen

Bridesmaids

Maid of
Honor

Ring
Bearer

Flower
Girl

BRIDE

Bride's
Father

Figure 9-1, Processional Formations
Christian Ceremony - Variation 2

Clergy/Officiant

GROOM

Best Man

Bridesmaids | Groomsmen

Maid of Honor

Ring Bearer

Flower Girl

BRIDE

Bride's Father

Figure 9-1, Processional Formations
Christian Ceremony - Variation 3

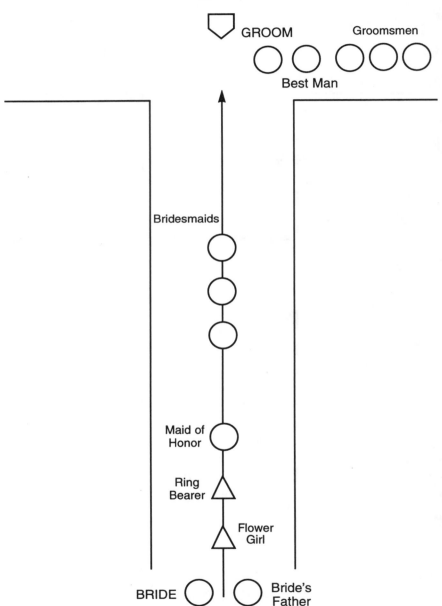

Figure 9-1, Processional Formations
Jewish Ceremony

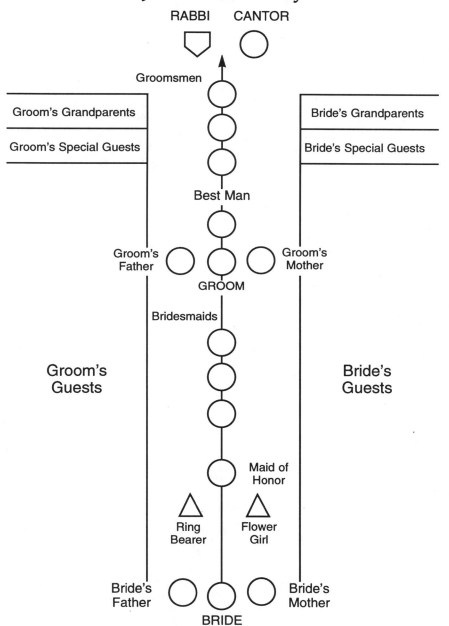

Figure 9-1, Processional Formations
Jewish Ceremony- Variation 1

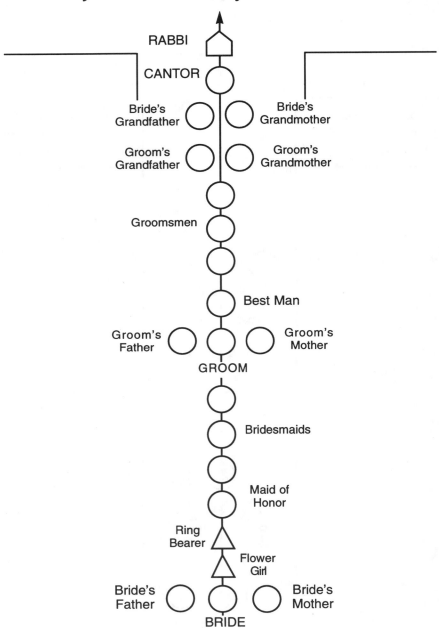

Figure 9-2, Altar Formations
Christian Ceremony

Clergy/Officiant

Maid of
Honor   BRIDE   GROOM   Best Man

Bridesmaids   Groomsmen

Flower   Ring
Girl   Bearer

Bride's
Father

83

Figure 9-2, Altar Formations
Christian Ceremony - Variation 1

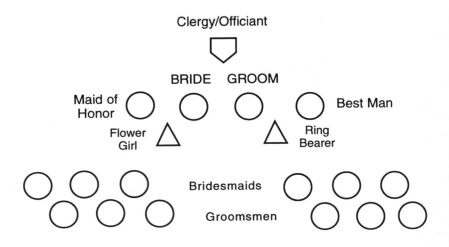

Figure 9-2, Altar Formations
Christian Ceremony - Variation 2

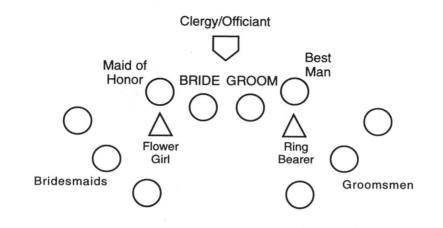

Clergy/Officiant

Maid of Honor   BRIDE   GROOM   Best Man

Flower Girl   Ring Bearer

Bridesmaids   Groomsmen

Figure 9-2, Altar Formations
Jewish Ceremony

RABBI   CANTOR

GROOM   BRIDE

Best
Man

Maid of
Honor

Groomsmen

Bridesmaids

Groom's   Groom's   Bride's   Bride's
Father   Mother   Father   Mother

Variation 1

RABBI   CANTOR

Best
Man

Maid of
Honor

Groomsmen

Groom's
Father

GROOM   BRIDE

Bride's
Mother

Bridesmaids

Groom's
Mother

Bride's
Father

Figure 9-3, Recessional Formations
Christian Ceremony

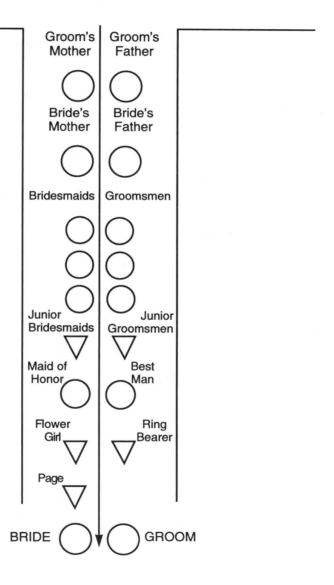

Clergy/Officiant

Groom's Mother | Groom's Father

Bride's Mother | Bride's Father

Bridesmaids | Groomsmen

Junior Bridesmaids | Junior Groomsmen

Maid of Honor | Best Man

Flower Girl | Ring Bearer

Page

BRIDE | GROOM

Figure 9-3, Recessional Formations
Christian Ceremony - Variation 1a and b

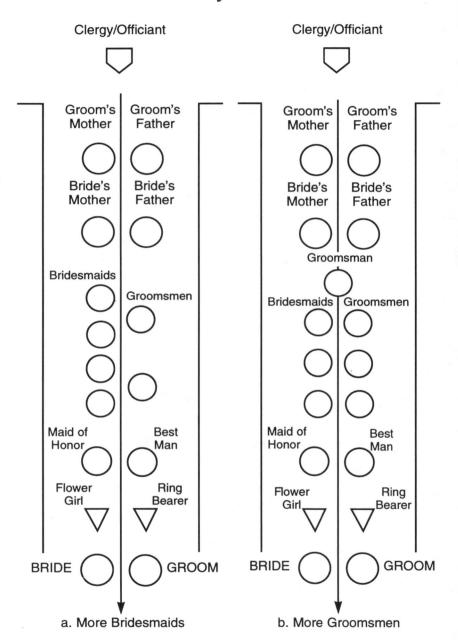

a. More Bridesmaids

b. More Groomsmen

Figure 9-3, Recessional Formations
Christian Ceremony - Variation 2

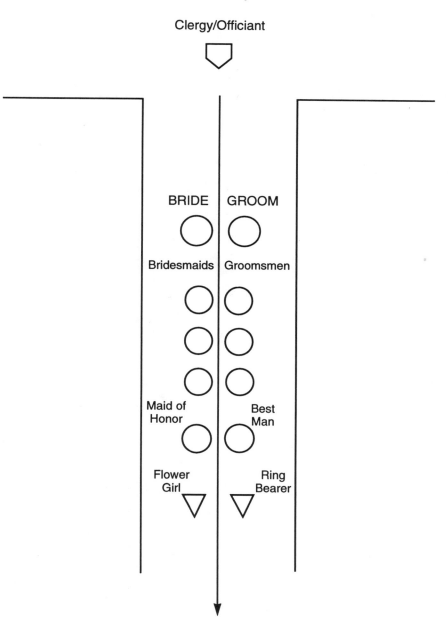

Clergy/Officiant

BRIDE   GROOM

Bridesmaids   Groomsmen

Maid of
Honor   Best
             Man

Flower   Ring
Girl   Bearer

Figure 9-3, Recessional Formations
Jewish Ceremony

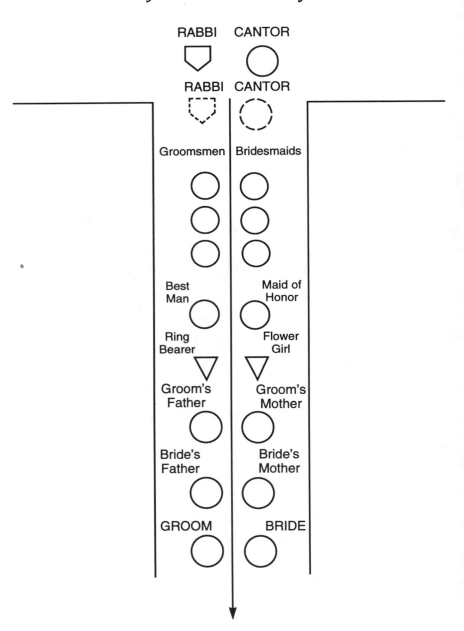

Figure 9-4, Receiving Line Formations

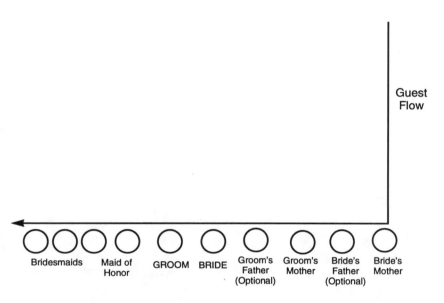

Variation 1
(If groom's parents do not know many of the guests)

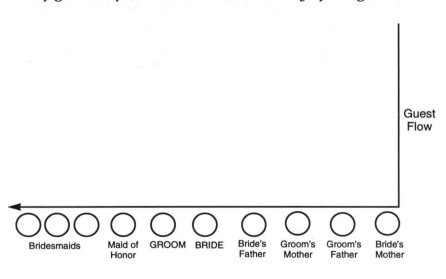

CHAPTER 10

How Do We Obtain the Marriage License?

Besides the religious and social requirements associated with marriage, each state has legislated legal requirements which must be met. The individual states have enacted laws governing marriageable ages (with and without consent), medical tests, waiting periods, residency, confidential weddings, and persons authorized to perform wedding services.

It is important to remember that a wedding is a public event. It is sanctioned by the state and, in many cases, by a religious authority. A wedding must conform to the laws of the state in which it is performed, whether it is sanctioned by a religious authority or not. This chapter discusses those legal requirements and provides guidelines on how to identify and satisfy the requirements.

A marriage is authorized by the state. By law, all states require a marriage license and each state has its own marriage licensing requirements. Therefore, you should contact the marriage license bureau or county clerk's office in the state and county in which you are planning to hold the ceremony. Listed below are some of the questions you should ask.

MARRIAGE LICENSE QUESTIONNAIRE

◆ What are the marriage license requirements in this state? _____

_____

◆ Do we need *certified* proof of age (birth certificate, immigration records, passports, etc.)? ☐ Yes ☐ No

◆ What is the age of majority for marriage in this state?

_____

(If you are under the age of majority) What type of proof of parental consent is required? _____

◆ Will we need proof of citizenship (birth certificate, immigration records, passports, etc.)? ☐ Yes ☐ No

◆ (If you were previously married) Do you need the date and location of the divorce or annulment and/or copies of the legal papers? ☐ Yes ☐ No

◆ Will blood tests be required? ☐ Yes ☐ No

If so, how long are the results valid? _____
How far in advance must the tests be scheduled to guarantee that you will have the results in time? _____

◆ Is there a minimum residence period within the state or county before a marriage license may be issued?
☐ Yes ☐ No

◆ Is there a waiting period before the license is valid?
☐ Yes ☐ No

◆ How long is the license valid? _____
What is the renewal procedure if the license expires?

_____

◆ What are the license fees? _____

Does the fee need to be paid with cash, a money order, or a cashier's check? (Specify) _____

Are personal checks and credit cards acceptable?

☐ Yes ☐ No

* When is the license bureau open? _____

At the marriage license bureau or county recorder's office, you will provide the required personal information and health certificate, pay the prescribed license fee, and receive the marriage license. After the ceremony has been performed, your witnesses (normally the best man and maid/matron of honor) and the clergy/officiant performing the ceremony sign the license, which is then returned to the state or county agency specified on the marriage license for recording and filing.

From a strictly legal point of view, marriage and divorce are the authority and responsibility of the state. Once a marriage license has been legally issued, the wedding ceremony performed by a legally sanctioned clergy/officiant, and the marriage license duly signed and recorded, the marriage is determined to have met all the state requirements. It is certified as "legal," no matter what objections a religion may have to the solemnization.

When two services are planned, such as a civil and a religious service or services in different locations, two separate licenses are sometimes required. If you are considering two services, you should contact the various license bureaus to find out the proper procedure.

Marriage License Bureau

Address:_____

_____

Telephone: ( )_____

Business Hours: _____ To: _____ Fee: $ _____

❏ Confidential Marriage

In some states, an unmarried couple who has been living together as husband and wife may be married by any authorized person without the necessity of a routine marriage license or health certificate. Records of such marriages are not open to public inspection except upon court order. In this manner, the state attempts to shield the couples and their children from the publicity of marriage recorded in the ordinary manner and to thereby encourage legalization of the relationship.

Depending upon the state, an authorization for the performance of the confidential marriage can be issued by the county clerk, clerk of the court, a judge in private chambers, and/or other designated officials. Upon performance of the marriage, the original confidential marriage certificate is signed by the person performing the ceremony and returned to the issuing agency. A copy of the certificate is given to the couple.

❏ Marriage Certificate

Some states and officiants will provide you with a marriage certificate as a memento of your wedding. Though not a legal document, the certificate confirms that the wedding took place.

❏ Officiants

There may be some confusion and misconceptions about who can legally officiate at a wedding. It cannot be assumed that persons authorized in one state will automatically be able to legally perform weddings in another state. Nor can it be assumed that the list of officials is limited to clergy members and judges.

Not only do states regulate marriage licensing criteria for the couple, they also enact laws/statutes/codes stipulating who is authorized to solemnize a wedding. The list of authorized officials can cover a broad spectrum, from clergy members and government officials to retired judges.

The following list from the California Civil Code, Section 4205, provides an example of the diversity of people who can be authorized to legally perform wedding services.

"Marriages may be solemnized by any judge or retired judge, commissioner or retired commissioner, or assistant commissioner of a court of record or justice court in the state, or by any priest, minister, or rabbi of any religious denomination, of the age of eighteen years or over or by any person authorized to do so under Section 4205.1. A marriage may also be solemnized by a judge who has resigned from office."

As with the marriage licensing laws, the individual states establish their own rules governing wedding officials. Some states have a formal licensing/certification process. Other states have designated minimum residency requirements which must be met before the clergy/officiant is authorized to legally conduct wedding services within the state. Still other states do not permit out-of-state clergy members to perform weddings.

In order to have a legally recognized wedding, you must abide by the laws of the state in which the wedding ceremony will be performed. Therefore, if you are planning to use out-of-state clergy (such as a family member, friend, relative, or current/past pastor) or if you are attempting to locate an authorized government official to perform a civil wedding service, you should do some research to determine what people are legally authorized to perform the ceremony.

If you plan to use clergy from out of state (different from the state in which the wedding is being performed), it is advisable that you contact the state/county marriage license bureau or county clerk's office. This contact should be made as soon as possible in your planning process to determine what the state requirements governing wedding officials are.

❐ Witnesses

The laws of various states require that a marriage be witnessed by at least two individuals of legal age. The marriage license provides for the signatures of the witnesses. In addition, the witnesses may be asked to sign the marriage certificate.

❐ Weddings in a Foreign Country

If you plan to be married in a foreign country, you should remember that a religious or civil ceremony must be conducted in accordance with the legal requirements of the foreign country. Therefore, you should contact the foreign country's embassy, consulate, or tourist office in the United States *before departing* to determine the specific marriage requirements of the country. Listed below are some of the questions that you should ask:

* Does this country have a residency requirement?
  ☐ Yes ☐ No

  If so, how long is the waiting period? _____

* What documentation do we need to present to the marriage registrar besides a valid United States passport?

  _____

  _____

* Does the required civil documentation which is presented to the marriage registrar have to be translated?
  ☐ Yes ☐ No

  If so, where can it be done? _____

  How long does it take?_____

  How much does it normally cost? _____

* What is the age of majority for marriage in the country?

  _____

What are the requirements for parental consent?

Does the consent have to be authenticated by a consular official of the foreign country in the United States?
☐ Yes ☐ No

• Does the country require an affidavit of eligibility to marry? ☐ Yes ☐ No

Can it be executed before a consular official of the foreign country in the United States? ☐ Yes ☐ No

If not, will it have to be prepared at the United States embassy or consulate in the country in which the wedding will occur? ☐ Yes ☐ No

• Does the country also require witnesses who will sign an affidavit that we are free to marry? ☐ Yes ☐ No

• Does the country require a blood test? ☐ Yes ☐ No

• Does marriage to a national of the foreign country automatically make the spouse either a citizen of the country or eligible to become a naturalized citizen of the country? ☐ Yes ☐ No

The automatic authorization of a second nationality does not affect United States citizenship. However, the application for citizenship by the individual or his/her authorized agent may cause the loss of United States citizenship. If you are planning to apply for a foreign citizenship, you should contact a United States Department of State, embassy, or consulate for information.

Information on obtaining a visa for a foreign spouse can be obtained from any office of the Immigration and Naturalization Service, United States embassies and consulates, or the Department of State, Visa Office, Washington, D.C. 20520-0113.

Some general information on marriage requirements for a limited number of countries can be obtained from the Office of Citizens Consular Services, Room 4817, Department of State, Washington, D.C. 20520. In addition, United States embassies and consulates abroad frequently have information about wedding requirements of the country in which they are located.

Marriages which are legally performed and valid in the foreign country are generally valid in the United States; however, it is a good idea to contact the marriage license agency or attorney general's office within your state of residency to determine whether the foreign marriage will be legally recognized within the state.

While United States diplomatic and consular officers cannot perform wedding ceremonies, they can authenticate foreign marriage documents for a fee.

As a rule, wedding services are not performed at the United States embassy or consulate offices. Therefore, you should contact either the United States Department of State, embassy, or consular office within the country you are planning to be married to obtain approval and make arrangements for the ceremony *before* finalizing your plans.

☐ Weddings in Paradise

The lure of a tropical wedding is drawing an increasing number of couples to our fiftieth state, Hawaii. Couples wanting to fulfill their dreams of a romantic sunset wedding on the beach with waves breaking in the background or among lush tropical plants and beautiful flowers beside a waterfall are planning weddings in Hawaii. The Islands' wedding business has become so big that most hotels and resorts offer complete wedding/honeymoon packages.

To prevent problems in obtaining a marriage license or finding a clergy/officiant when you arrive on the Islands, you should find out what the marraige license and clergy/officiant requirements are ahead of time. You should contact the Hawaii State Department of Health, Office of Health Status Monitoring, Marriage License Section, 1250 Punchbowl

Street, Honolulu, Hawaii 96813, or call them at (808) 586-4544. The telephone numbers for the local registrars on the other islands are: Hawaii (808) 933-4327; Kauai (808) 241-3495; Maui (808) 243-5313; Molokai (808) 567-6161; and Lanai (808) 565-6411.

The requirements for getting married in the Hawaiian Islands are as follows. However, even though the information was current when this edition was printed, you should check with the licensing section to determine whether any of the requirements have been updated.

♦ Both parties must appear at the marriage license office in person, complete the Marriage License Application Form, and pay the license fee (in cash). Office hours are 8:00 a.m. to 4:00 p.m., Monday through Friday. There is an office on all the major islands.

♦ The marriage license is valid for thirty days from date of issuance.

♦ There is no residence or U.S. citizenship requirement.

♦ Legal age for both males and females is eighteen years old. With written consent of the parents, legal guardian, or family court, couples may be married at sixteen years of age. For younger couples, proof of age, in the form of a certified copy of a birth certificate or baptismal certificate, may be required. Plan on taking one or the other with you if applicable. Driver's licenses or identification cards are not acceptable.

♦ Brides-to-be must submit a premarital health certificate for rubella screening signed by a licensed physician at the time of applying for the license. The certificate form may be either a State of Hawaii Department of Health form or a form from a state having similar requirements. The certificate must be signed by both the physician and the director of the government-approved laboratory where the blood test was performed.

- ◆ Weddings must be performed by a clergy/officant licensed in the state of Hawaii.

❑ Weddings at Sea

In the absence of any state law to the contrary, marriages performed at sea by a ship's captain are legal. Therefore, you should contact your county marriage license bureau to determine if the state in which you reside acknowledges weddings performed at sea. You should also contact the ship/cruise line to determine whether they authorize ship captains or chaplains to perform wedding ceremonies.

❑ Other Legal Considerations

In addition to the state laws requiring a marriage license, there are many other legal and important documents which will need to be modified as a result of a marriage. You will either have to change your surname or add your spouse to appropriate documents. These changes should be made either before your wedding or immediately upon return from your honeymoon. The documents include such items as: bank accounts, credit cards, driver's license, employment records, insurance (automobile, health, and life), loan accounts, medical records, memberships, passports, property titles, social security card, vehicle title and registration, voter's registration, and wills. You will also need to file a change of address at the post office.

You should note that updated social security cards can take up to two or three months to obtain. You cannot change some documents (e.g. your driver's license) without the updated social security card.

❑ Prenuptial Agreements

Prenuptial agreements are becoming more prominent — particularly in remarriages. It is important for both parties to be as educated as possible in the legal issues surrounding marriage. You and your future spouse should know and discuss your legal rights in a marriage relationship *before* you marry.

A prenuptial agreement, whether it is signed or not, can be a positive communication tool for clarifying and resolving important issues concerning children, concessions, dreams, employment, family, home, money, personal space, possessions, promises, rights, and problems that might arise from those issues. It can be a covenant or commitment concerning what you have agreed to do in the marriage. In fact, some wedding ceremonies, such as the Islamic and Jewish, focus upon the public reading of a marriage contract as part of the service.

CHAPTER 11

What Type of Wedding Ceremony Do We Want?

The guiding principles of planning a wedding are shaped from your shared traditions, expectations, and desires. People treasure an image of a wedding; and after it is over, they should fondly remember the feelings it evoked and the special meaning it conveyed.

The question of whether to have a religious or civil ceremony is an issue which you will need to discuss and decide upon based on your basic values, attitudes, and philosophies of life. The ceremony should reflect your religious commitment as well as your personal values. The religious quality of your ceremony can be a cementing factor in your married life.

In order to create the most meaningful, enriching experience possible, you should give considerable thought to choosing the type of service, style, and setting of your wedding service. These items may be interchanged or modified depending upon your particular desires.

Though services do differ, the differences in many cases are slight. Such differences may simply be the result of your attitudes or philosophies regarding weddings. Consequently, wedding ceremonies fall into a number of patterns as described in the remainder of this section.

☐ Types of Services

Traditional

A traditional wedding ceremony maintains a basic, uniform style of formality and degree of decorum. It reflects society's accepted customs and etiquette. It is based upon an established pattern of common practice or heritage. As such, what is "traditional" is affected by religious, cultural, and geographical influences.

Modified

A modified wedding ceremony follows the basic pattern of a traditional ceremony, but is tailored, in an acceptable manner, to accommodate special items that the couple wishes to personalize in the ceremony, such as the preparing and reciting of special readings or different religious and/or cultural customs.

Contemporary

A contemporary or nontraditional wedding ceremony substitutes and mixes the elements of a traditional ceremony in an original way. It is designed to be flexible so it incorporates current lifestyles and personal expression, yet it still reflects the very special social event that a wedding is.

❏ Styles

Very Formal — Traditional

A very formal wedding is usually held in a church, temple, or luxury hotel. It is normally held at noon, late afternoon, or in the evening, and has 200 or more guests in attendance. There are between four and twelve bridesmaids in floor-length dresses, one usher for every twenty-five to fifty guests, a maid or matron of honor, a best man, a flower girl, a ring bearer, and pages. Engraved or printed invitations with separate reception invitations enclosed are mailed to the guests. Long dresses are worn by the bride's and groom's mothers. The bride wears a satin or lace gown with a cathedral or chapel train and a full-length veil. If the gown is short-sleeved or sleeveless, long gloves are worn. The bride carries an elaborate bouquet or flower-trimmed prayer book. The style, length, and color of the bride's attendants' attire should complement the bride's gown and carry out her wedding theme.

Formal attire is worn by the groom and the other men in the wedding party. For a very formal daytime wedding, the groom and male attendants normally wear a black or gray cutaway coat with gray and black striped trousers, gray waistcoat, formal wing-collared white shirt, a striped ascot, gray gloves, and black shoes and socks. As optional accessories, the men may wear gray spats and black silk hats.

For a very formal evening wedding, the groom and male attendants would wear a black tailcoat tuxedo or a dinner jacket with black striped trousers, white waist coat, white shirt with winged collar and French cuffs, white bow tie, white gloves, black patent leather shoes, and black socks.

When the wedding is to be a military ceremony, the attire is the full dress uniform.

Formal — Traditional

A formal wedding includes many of the above elements, but it may be held in a hotel, restaurant, banquet room, private club, or home, in addition to a religious setting. It may be held at any hour, include at least 100 guests, and is personalized with the couple's vows, music, and/or readings. There are between two and eight bridesmaids in long dresses, and one usher for every fifty guests. Engraved or printed invitations are mailed, but reception cards may not be included. Long or street-length dresses are worn by the mothers. The bride is attired in a less elaborate gown with a chapel or sweep train, a hem- or finger-tip-length veil or veiled hat, and short gloves with short-sleeved gowns. The bride also carries a simpler bouquet.

The groom, the male attendants, and the fathers of the bride and groom wear formal attire. In a formal daytime wedding, the groom and male attendants could wear a black or gray contoured long or short jacket, striped trousers, white shirt with turned-down collar and French cuffs, striped four-in-hand tie, gray gloves, and black shoes and socks.

For a formal evening wedding, the groom and male attendants wear black or charcoal gray dinner jackets with

107

matching striped trousers, white pleated front shirt with turned-down collar and French cuffs, coordinating vest or cummerbund, bow tie, and black shoes and socks.

Semiformal — Traditional

A semiformal wedding is usually held in a nonreligious setting, normally the same location where the reception is held. There are one or two attendants. The ceremony may be held at any time, with morning, early afternoon, and late evening being the most popular times. There are fewer than 100 guests. Aisle ribbons and aisle carpets are normally omitted. Single engraved or printed invitations to both ceremony and reception are sent. Street-length or cocktail-length dresses are appropriate attire for the couple's mothers, while the bridesmaids wear street-length or cocktail-length dresses. The bride typically selects an elaborate street-length or simple floor-length gown without a train. She wears a short veil, a hat, or flowers in her hair. She carries a simpler bouquet.

The men wear dark suits, dinner jackets, or contemporary formal suits. Traditionally, during the day, the groom and male attendants wear solid dark suits, plain white shirts, four-in-hand ties, and black shoes and socks. A white tuxedo jacket, a white shirt with a white turned-down collar, a bow tie, and a vest or cummerbund may be worn instead.

The men's evening semiformal attire would be contemporary formal suits or dinner jackets with dress shirts, bow ties, vests, or cummerbunds.

Informal — Traditional

An informal wedding can take place in a home, chapel, judge's chambers, club, restaurant, or outdoors. Although it is usually a daytime ceremony, it may be held at any time. Handwritten or personal invitations to both ceremony and reception are sent. The wedding party consists of the bride, the groom, the best man, and the maid of honor. Fewer than fifty guests are in attendance. Guests may be directed to the wedding area by the bride's mother, the honor attendant, a relative, or a close friend. There is usually not a processional or recessional, although the bride may be escorted by her father or the groom. After the ceremony, the couple turns to greet their guests. Street-length dresses are appropriate attire for the mothers, the honor attendant, and the bride. The bride's flowers are worn, not carried. Business suits for the groom, the best man, and the couple's fathers are acceptable.

Nontraditional

Nontraditional ceremonies maintain the basic styles of formality, but substitute or mix elements according to the desires of the couple. Nontraditional ceremonies are original and do not fit a particular formula. Today, the etiquette governing nontraditional ceremonies is flexible enough to meet all your needs for privacy or personal expression.

Bridal Etiquette

You should adapt your attire to the ceremony location and should not buy your gown until you have decided where the ceremony will be held.

You may wear a long, white gown no matter what your age or number of previous marriages. In practice, many previously married brides fulfill their dreams for an elaborate wedding dress and train. However, if you are an older first marriage bride or a previously married bride, you may select an informal bridal gown in a long or tea length. An older bride may choose a three-piece suit, knee-length cocktail dress, or floor length gown. All are appropriate as long as they suit your wedding style.

❑ Settings

Church/Temple

One of the most responsive and attractive places to hold your service is in your church or temple, where the symbols and atmosphere add to the meaning and purpose of your pending nuptials.

If you are considering a church or temple, do not be concerned that the sanctuary may be too large, since the size of the sanctuary does not necessarily bear upon the service. If the number of guests is small, they may be concentrated in the front of the sanctuary and need not be concerned about the empty pews behind them.

A wedding chapel also provides a religious atmosphere for couples of different faiths, or for those couples without a specific church affiliation.

Club/Hotel

A club, hotel, winery, or historical site wedding treats the processional, altar procedures, and recessional in much the same manner as a home wedding, and can be very dignified and beautiful.

At these sites, the bride's mother may greet the guests as they arrive. Other members of the family who are not in the wedding party may mingle with the guests before the ceremony.

In a smaller, simpler, more intimate ceremony, the bride may choose to greet the guests and step up to the altar naturally and easily with the groom at her side.

Cruise Ship

Couples wishing to be married aboard a cruise ship, with the high seas providing a beautiful backdrop, should contact the cruise companies before making their plans. Many cruise companies either do not perform wedding services or restrict them to prior to departing or immediately after returning from the cruise. Others require that the wedding ceremony be performed by a bona fide clergy person and only allow the ship's captain to renew vows.

Foreign Country

If you will be married in a foreign country, your planning will be more challenging. A wedding in a foreign country must be conducted in accordance with the requirements of that country. You should contact the foreign country's embassy, consulate, or tourist office in the United States to determine specific marriage requirements. Chapter 10 has a more detailed discussion of the requirements for weddings held in a foreign country.

Home

The home is an appropriate setting for an intimate, charming, and sentimental wedding. The bride's mother may stand near the door to greet the guests as they arrive, or she may wait with the bride and her attendants until just before the ceremony. If she waits with the bride, she may delegate a relative or close friend to greet the guests.

In a home wedding, ushers are normally more honorary than active. However, they should be available to escort each of the mothers and guests needing assistance.

The procession is usually modified. Depending upon the size and layout of the home, the bridesmaids, the honor attendant, and the bride with her father may enter from an adjacent room or down a staircase. As an alternative, the bride may enter alone and meet her father near the entrance to the wedding room, at which time her father escorts her to the groom's side. Prior to the wedding day, the couple should make sure that there is sufficient room for the bride's wedding gown and all its trappings, as well as the wedding party.

It is not unusual to omit an altar in a home wedding. However, an altar can be easily improvised, borrowed from a church, or rented.

A recession is normally not necessary. At the end of the ceremony, the groom kisses the bride, the officiant congratulates the couple, the couple turns toward the guests and are introduced as husband and wife by the clergy/officiant. The guests then gather around to give the couple their best wishes.

Outdoor/Garden

During the warmer months, outdoor or garden weddings can be beautiful. An open-air wedding ceremony at a beach, park, private garden or other such setting offers an alternative to the traditional church wedding. An outdoor/garden wedding may be formal, semiformal, or informal, depending upon the style of the wedding attire.

When planning an outdoor or garden wedding, you should consider weather (rain, temperature, and wind), ability to hear the service, and distracting vehicular and/or human traffic. You should also check with your clergy/officiant to make sure that he/she will perform an open-air ceremony. And finally, you should find out what the rules and restrictions are for the site.

The procedures for the service are similar to those for a wedding in the home. If you wish to have a procession, remember that an aisle runner may be laid to outline the way to the altar and to protect the train of the bride's dress (if it has one). But please use caution, as the runner can hide uneven ground which can cause stumbles and falls. In addition, make sure that it is securely anchored to prevent it from blowing in a wind.

Music for an open-air ceremony can be a real challenge since acoustics are different. Special arrangements may have to be made to provide electrical power and to protect the musicians and their instruments/equipment from the elements.

Flower arrangements should be adequately secured to prevent them from being blown over and sufficiently watered to keep them looking fresh.

When preparing for an outdoor wedding, observe where the sun will be at the time of the wedding, spray for insects before the service, and make sure automatic sprinkler systems have been shut off. You should consider both your comfort and that of your guests when arranging the site, paying careful attention to such things as providing a canopy for shade, seating arrangements, distance from parking and rest rooms, conditions of paths or trails to the site, and arrangements for wedding party and guest parking and/or admission fees. It is also a good idea to have an alternative site, such as the bride's parent's home, in case of bad weather.

□ Special Ceremonies

Candlelight Ceremony

A dramatic addition to a wedding ceremony may be created with the romantic glow of candles. You should, however, check local fire officials to determine if there are regulations as to the proper number and placement of the candles.

A candlelight service is usually associated with a late afternoon or evening ceremony or a dark site. Therefore, placement of the candles is very important. As an example, candles on stands may be placed at the ends of the aisles and/or on the window sills. Candelabras may be used at the altar area. Special effects, such as dimming all the interior lights while spotlighting the altar area, are very dramatic. The couple should meet early with site representatives to discuss the possibilities and limitations if candles are to be used.

For a candlelight service, two ushers, special designees, or representatives of the site proceed slowly up the aisles, lighting the candles as the interior lights are dimmed prior to seating the bride's mother and before the procession begins. The candles may also be lit by honored guests or ushers during the ceremony. Or, as a variation, the candles may be lit as soon as the ushers arrive, prior to the seating of any guests.

During the ceremony itself, the lighting of the unity candle can add symbolism. Throughout the service, a candle in the center of the altar area remains unlit. When the clergy/officiant pronounces you husband and wife, you carry lit candles to the altar to light the unity candle. The unity candle may be used to indicate the joining of your family, to symbolize an interfaith wedding, and/or to create a new blended family if you were previously married. You then extinguish your two candles, leaving the unity candle burning to represent the new union. Or the side candles may remain lit to symbolize your individual personalities which remain within the marriage relationship. In a reaffirmation of vows, the candle can symbolize that the flame of love is still burning.

After the recessional and before the guests are directed out, the ushers can slowly proceed toward the altar, extinguishing the candles as the interior lights are raised. Or, as a variation, the candles may be extinguished after the guests leave.

Civil Ceremony

The option of a wedding ceremony outside of the church is available. Most civil ceremonies are performed by a legally qualified person in a courthouse, a judge's chambers, a justice of the peace's home, or any other site of your choice. If it is a large ceremony performed at a home or in a club, the procedures are the same as for a religious ceremony of like formality.

A civil ceremony normally has less religious language. It is common to have a quiet and intimate civil ceremony during the day with the reception at night.

Since laws vary from state to state, it is a good idea to contact the marriage license bureau in the county where the wedding is to be performed to determine what officials can perform civil marriage ceremonies. Chapter 10 has a more detailed discussion of wedding officiants.

Clergy Ceremony

When the groom is a clergy member, the ceremony is generally either performed in the bride's church or synagogue and/or by her clergy. When the bride is a member of the groom's congregation, either the groom's superior or another clergy of equal position performs the ceremony. The groom may either wear his clerical clothes or other attire appropriate to the style of the wedding.

When the bride is a clergy member, the ceremony may either be held in her church or synagogue and/or performed by her superior or another clergy of her choice. Like the groom, the bride may either wear her clerical clothes or other appropriate attire.

If one of the parents is a clergy member, he or she may perform the ceremony. If it is the father of the bride, another person may escort the bride down the aisle.

Double Wedding

A double wedding is normally formal, with each couple having their own wedding party attire in coordinated colors and styles. The couples should make sure that the wedding site selected has ample space.

The two grooms walk together behind the clergy/officiant and take their places side by side, each with his own best man behind him, the groom of the first bride standing nearer the aisle. Both sets of ushers can lead the procession. The bridesmaids, honor attendant, flower girl, and bride on her father's arm enter. The second set of attendants and second bride enter in the same manner. The attendants separate, with the attendants for the first bride on the left and the attendants for the second bride on the right. The two couples stand side by side in front of the clergy/officiant, with the first bride on the left. Each couple completes each section of the ceremony in turn. The final blessing is given to both couples at the same time. The recession is led by the first couple, then the second, followed by the alternating members of the wedding party (e.g. first honor attendant, second honor attendant, etc.).

If the brides are sisters, the oldest usually enters and leaves first. The father may escort both daughters down the aisle, or another relative (brother or mother) may escort one. However, the father may give both daughters away. He stands behind the first bride until he gives her away, then moves behind the second bride to give her away.

If the brides are friends, each father gives his own daughter in marriage.

Military Wedding

A groom in any branch of the military may be married in uniform, but only commissioned officers in full dress uniform may carry swords/sabers. Reserve officers do not have military weddings unless they are on active duty. Boutonnieres are not worn with uniforms, but large medals are worn with dress uniforms.

If the bride and her attendants are in the military, they may either wear traditional dress or their uniforms. If both the bride and groom are in the military, the entire wedding party may be in uniform.

The military procession follows standard procedures. It is the recession that is distinctive and truly memorable for the guests. The arch of steel is formed by the groom's fellow officers who also serve as ushers. It may be formed either inside the church, outside on the steps, or both. The head usher issues the commands to center face, to arch sabers/draw swords, and finally to return them to carry position. When the arch is formed, each groomsman raises the saber/sword in his right hand with the cutting edge facing up. After the bride and groom have passed under the arch, followed by the maid of honor and best man and the bridesmaids by twos, the sabers/swords are returned to their scabbards. It is equally correct to have the groomsmen escort the bridesmaids in the recessional after the bride and groom have passed under the arch.

As a rule, only the bride's father is in civilian attire unless he is in the military also. It is not required that all the groomsmen be in the military. Those who are not should wear traditional formal attire. The bride, her attendants, the couple's mothers, and guests should dress appropriately for the hour and season of the wedding.

Decorations may include the national and bride's/ groom's regimental colors or unit standards arranged with the flowers at the altar. The flags may be crossed or stand separately.

Reaffirming Vows

Reaffirmation of wedding vows is a recent ceremony that began about ten years ago. The reaffirmation service may take the form of a classic, traditional wedding service, or it may be a simple gathering of family and friends at home, where the couple and guests share significant, sentimental experiences. It is a time when you announce that you still want to be married to your spouse by repeating the vows that first united you and by exchanging your original rings. Or you may have an entirely different style of service to express how your feelings for each other have grown.

Many couples choose to recreate their wedding day, complete with original dress and attendants. Others have a clergy renew their vows during an anniversary party. Other couples use the opportunity to completely redesign their ceremony.

There is no established service for this purpose, and the ceremony is not a legal act. Since it is a reaffirmation to celebrate the fulfillment of the wedding promises made earlier, the couple does not need a license or a clergy/legal officiant in order to pledge their everlasting commitment to each other. Also, the presiding person does not "pronounce" the couple as husband and wife. Some churches have an annual event in which couples may reaffirm their marriages.

A reaffirmation may be held to celebrate a renewal of wedding vows, to receive the church's blessing for an earlier civil wedding, or to celebrate a significant milestone in a marriage, such as the tenth anniversary.

❑ Remarriage

Society's views on remarriage have changed dramatically over the years. Rigid standards have faded away and have been replaced by a new sense of flexibility and openness. There are no longer rigid social restrictions against remarriage.

The new marriage is a time for rejoicing in a new beginning. Therefore, you and your families may choose the wedding style and size that you wish based upon common sense and your personal style.

With more remarriages, a growing number of couples approach the altar with ambivalence. You should remember that your remarriage deserves as much, or more, planning and attention as your previous wedding. However, you now have the opportunity to plan a ceremony that is more imaginative and innovative.

It is a time for you and your fiancé to plan together for a wedding to suit your style and budget. Since it is a remarriage, you should plan to pay for it yourselves. Do not ask your parents for financial help; but if they offer to help, you must decide whether to accept it and, if you do, to determine what expenses it will be used for.

Whenever children are involved, you have to make decisions and compromises between your preferences and the needs of the children. You should tell them about your plans as soon as possible, especially if they are young and/or will be part of the new household. Remember that including children in the wedding is not restricted solely to their role in the ceremony itself. It is vital to include your children in all aspects of your wedding planning. Be sure to let your ex-spouse know of your plans ahead of time, however, in case he or she may object to involving the children.

The role of your children in the ceremony should be determined by the size and style of the ceremony. You may wish to include them in the wedding party so they may stand with you at the altar, or you may ask them to read a special verse. It is important that your children's feelings not be ignored during the planning and last-minute rush of activities before the ceremony.

While society's attitude toward remarriage has become more lenient, it is a good idea to contact your clergy member as soon as possible to determine whether there are any denominational rules that would prevent you from having a traditional service or the type of service you are planning.

While it is permissible for a widow to be given away a second time, a divorced woman is rarely given away a second time. In either situation, you may prefer to have the person escorting you down the aisle "support" or "bless" the marriage.

CHAPTER 12

What About Religious Practices and Wedding Traditions?

The United States has a rich heritage of religious traditions. Each religion has customs associated with its wedding ceremony. These customs have evolved over time and have been adapted to accommodate changing values and cultural blending.

A wedding is a highly ritualized, spiritual event. Wedding services cover a wide variety of religious convictions and practices. While wedding ceremonies share some similarities, there are more differences among the religions. Differences in religious beliefs, interpretations, and customs/traditions are reflected in their wedding ceremonies.

This chapter describes some of the significant variations in wedding attitudes, rules, and practices encountered among the variety of major religions within the United States. See Table 12-1 (on page 127) for a presentation of the wedding order of service for some of the major religions.

☐ Religious Practices

Bahai

Members of the Bahai faith must have a Bahai wedding ceremony. The principle foundation for the institution of marriage within the Bahai faith is the expression of love and unity. The major emphasis is placed upon the preparations for marriage, commitments and responsibilities, and family life.

As such, a Bahai wedding ceremony itself has minimal requirements to follow.

The basic Bahai wedding ceremony must be very simple. It includes the recitation of a verse and the reading of selected writings. The ceremony does not follow a prescribed, uniform format. However, the couple may add items if they wish, as long as the items are in keeping with the faith.

The bride and groom are required to repeat the verse, "We will all, verily, abide by the will of God," before two witnesses. The witnesses must be chosen from within the faith by either the couple or the Spiritual Assembly. Since the Bahai do not have ministers, a Bahai member of the Spiritual Assembly officiates.

The Bahai openly allow interfaith marriages. However, when two wedding ceremonies (i.e. another religious or civil ceremony as well as a Bahai ceremony) are to be performed, they must be performed on the same day and with the same amount of respect.

Bahai law does not restrict the ceremony to a Bahai assembly hall. The only restriction on where the Bahai ceremony can be conducted is that it cannot be held in another religion's place of worship.

While the Bahai consider marriage a sacred and binding relationship and view divorce as a reprehensible act which should be resorted to only in exceptional circumstances, they do allow it, recognizing civil divorces and permitting remarriage.

Buddhism

As with other major religions, there are many variables in Buddhism depending upon the individual countries in which it is practiced. In some countries, a wedding is not a religious ceremony. In others, the Buddhist priest is called into the wedding ceremony, where he reads an extract from Buddhist Scriptures and prays for a blessing on the couple, who are sprinkled with holy water. After further prayers and feasting, the wedding is complete.

For the Shinto, the priest officiates at the ceremony that brings the bride into the family of the groom. Ancestors are honored in the ritual by bowing, ringing bells, and offering food before family ancestral shrines. The bride wears a ceremonial kimono. No vows are repeated. After the ceremony, sips of sake are exchanaged with the parents, both to honor them and to acknowledge their formal acceptance of the marriage.

Catholic (Roman)

In the Catholic church, the wedding service is an act of holiness. In accordance with the Constitution of the Sacred Liturgy, the wedding takes place during a Mass held especially for the wedding.

The church may require the couple to show evidence of baptism performed within at least six months of the wedding date, a record of confirmation, and a letter of free state issued by the parishes for both parties. The couple may be asked to participate in a prematrimonial investigation conducted by the priest to make certain they enter marriage freely and that they fully consent to each other. They may also be requested to attend premarital conferences.

When both the bride and groom are Catholic, the "banns" are either announced from the pulpit at mass or published in the church bulletin on three consecutive Sundays before the ceremony in the parishes of both. Exceptions to this are interfaith marriages, marriages of older couples, and when the priest chooses to dispense with it.

A Catholic bride must receive permission from her parish priest in order to be married in another parish. The priest performing the ceremony needs proof of baptism and assurance that both parties are free to marry.

In interfaith marriages, priests are encouraged to welcome requests for mixed marriages, and to cooperate with the clergy of the non-Catholic partner. The non-Catholic partner normally is not required to sign any papers or make any promises to rear children from the marriage as Catholic, but that decision is up to the local parish. The non-Catholic partner does not have to be baptized, but must be free to marry in the Catholic church, meaning that the Catholic partner may have to request dispensation. While Catholic weddings are normally not performed outside the church, interfaith marriages may be conducted in non-Catholic churches with a priest assisting. An interfaith marriage performed by two clergy may be conducted in a Catholic church.

The marriage of divorced people generally is not allowed within the Catholic church unless the previous marriage has been annulled by the Catholic church.

Weddings are not normally performed at certain times: in the evening, during Advent, on Holy Thursday, Good Friday and Holy Saturday, or during regular Mass.

Christian Scientist

Marriage is the legal and moral provision for generations among humankind. The union of man and woman constitutes completeness.

Since Readers of the Christian Science faith are not ordained, the service may be performed by either an ordained minister or a civil authority.

Church of Jesus Christ of Latter Day Saints (Mormon)

Mormons perform two types of wedding services. The first is performed in the temple upon approval of the members of the Holy Priesthood. The second is a civil service performed by a bishop or other legal authority outside the temple.

If both the bride and groom are in "good standing" with the church, which means that they meet religious qualifications, have tithed, and have attended church the past two years, they can be married in the temple.

For a wedding in the temple, the condition of being in good standing applies to the parents and guests as well. If they do not meet the conditions, they cannot witness the wedding in the temple.

If either of the couple is not in good standing or is not a member of the Mormon church, the couple may be married in what is termed a civil wedding. The civil wedding service is still recognized by the church as a religious ceremony. It is usually performed by the bishop in the visitors' center. Members of the couple's family and guests can attend this service.

Interfaith marriages are permitted.

Eastern Rite (Orthodox)

The Orthodox churches in the United States have retained more of the traditional manners and practices than the churches in some of the other countries of the world. In the Orthodox faith, marriage is a sacrament. The wedding takes place in a church — usually in the afternoon or early evening. Ceremonies are not held during any season of fasting, during the eve of select holy days, during the Lenten season, during the week after Easter, or during the time of Advent to the Feast of Epiphany.

The couple meets with their priest and presents their baptism and christmation (christening) certificates. The pastor then permits the announcement of the marriage banns.

Prior to the wedding, the bride and groom participate in the Sacrament of Penance and Holy Communion in order to cleanse themselves of sins.

The traditional ceremony is long and steeped in symbolism in which each act has a special meaning. Music is restricted. The maid of honor and best man have more responsibilities during the ceremony than in a typical Protestant ceremony. Many of the elements of the service are repeated three times to signify the Holy Trinity.

Formerly, the betrothal and wedding services were conducted separately. In current church practices, however, it is celebrated immediately before the wedding service at the narthex (back) of the church. The betrothal service includes the blessing and exchanging of rings three times. The rings are blessed and laid on the altar table. The priest takes the rings in his hand, makes the sign of the cross over the couple's heads, and repeats a betrothal prayer three times. The priest places the rings on the right hand as the hand of blessing and of power. The best man exchanges the rings three times, taking the groom's ring and putting it on the bride's hand and vice versa.

After the betrothal service, the couple follows the priest to the center of the church to begin the Order of Marriage (crowning). The couple is given candles to symbolize their mutual burning love and the light of their future Christian life together. The flame also symbolizes prayer and reminds the couple that their love for God must burn as hot as the flame of the candle.

Two crowns are placed over the couple's heads to signify their coronation into a family realm. The crowns also symbolize the crowns of martyrdom, since every true marriage involves immeasurable mutual sacrifice. The groom and bride are crowned to be good rulers of a new family, and to rule with Christian love, wisdom, and humility. In addition, the crowns are signs of the glory and honor with which God will crown them in the kingdom of heaven if they live their lives according to God's laws.

After the Epistle and the Gospel are read, a common cup of wine in remembrance of Communion is shared by the couple (each drinking three times) to symbolize the joys and the sorrows they will share.

At the bridal procession, or "dance of Isaiah," the couple's *koumbaros* (sponsor) introduces them into married life. The bride, groom, and sponsor are led around a ceremonial table with their right hands joined. During the procession, three hymns are sung. At the close of the ceremony, after the veneration of the cross, the bridal couple, followed by the entire congregation, proceeds from the church.

Remarriages are blessed by the Orthodox church rather than being sacramental.

Interfaith marriages are forbidden by canon law, though consideration of such marriages is given in certain cases. Marriage to a unbaptized person is not allowed, however, nor is a non-Orthodox clergy permitted to participate in the service.

✦ *Greek Orthodox*

The standard wedding procession where the father gives the bride away is customary in Greek Orthodox services. The bride wears a face veil. Guests are allowed to sit during less sacred parts of the service. Crowns are placed on the heads of the bridal couple. The best man may also drink from the common cup, which is a local custom within the United States and not a practice of the church. Friends of the family stand on the church steps and distribute packets of candy to the other guests.

✦ *Russian Orthodox*

The wedding party is met at the vestibule door by the priest, and the bride is given away before the procession proceeds. The bride does not have to wear a face veil. The honor attendant and best man hold the crowns above the heads of the couple (periodically being relieved by the other attendants/groomsmen).

Hinduism

A Hindu wedding ceremony begins with *havan*, which is the worship of the fire god, Agni. The Hindu believe that fire represents the sun god, without whom there can be no life on earth. The sun god treats all as equals and passes through both clean as well as filthy elements, yet retains a pure nature.

Gifts are exchanged. Toward the end of the ceremony, the couple circles the fire god seven times and exchanges a new vow after completing each circle. They exchange vows of mutual love and respect, promising to share their joys and sorrows, help and consult each other, respect their elders, bring up their children with love and devotion, and discharge family and social obligations with sincerity and zeal.

Jewish

The Jewish wedding service represents the blending of legal and religious practices. No single guideline or procedure applies to all Jewish weddings, since there are differences among the Orthodox, Conservative, and Reform segments and each has different requirements and procedures.

Jewish law does not stipulate that a rabbi must be present at a wedding. In fact, a rabbi has no functions in Judaism that any other Jew could not perform. But the rabbi's role as the learned interpreter and representative of the Jewish tradition holds deep emotional and spiritual meaning to most Jews. Symbolically, the rabbi's participation in the wedding service appears to sanctify the marriage. As a rule, rabbis will not perform mixed marriages.

In Jewish life, marriage is a *mitzvah* — a commandment contained in the Torah. The wedding service is an act of *kiddush*, or sanctification. Jewish weddings may be performed at any time except on the Sabbath, holy days, a festival (Passover, *Shavu'ot*, and *Sukkot*), and other special times, such as three weeks during midsummer, and recently *Yom ha-Sho'ah* (Holocaust Day). Orthodox tradition also forbids weddings during the seven weeks beginning with Passover and ending with *Shavu'ot* (Festival of Weeks). Reform rabbis do not follow these restrictions.

Most weddings are celebrated on Saturday evening or Sunday and are normally not held in synagogues or temples.

Formal betrothals may precede marriage by six to twelve months or more. On the Sabbath before the wedding, the Reader refers to the wedding in a chanted address. Fasting normally takes place on the wedding morning, with the wedding taking place in the afternoon. While the bride and groom are not permitted to see each other before the wedding ceremony begins, the groom, as a prewedding ritual, may look under the bride's veil to assure that she is his betrothed. This tradition relates to the time of Jacob, when he discovered that his uncle, Laban, had tricked him into marrying Leah, who was behind the veil rather than Rachel.

The wedding is customarily performed under a *chuppah* (a bridal canopy of silk or velvet about two yards square, or a large prayer shawl) that symbolizes the ancient bridal chamber of consummation, the shelter from the open sky in ancient times, and the home in which the couple will live. At least ten adults must be present at the wedding. The bride stands to the groom's right under the canopy with the rabbi facing them, their parents standing behind them, the honor attendant positioned to the bride's right, and the best man positioned to the groom's left. The bridesmaids and ushers are on opposite sides of the canopy.

The service begins with a betrothal ceremony, then an introductory blessing. During the service, the rabbi stands next to a small table covered with a white cloth and set with cups of ritual wine and a glass wrapped in white silk.

After the blessing, the groom sips from the glass of wine and passes it to the bride. The bride and groom share the cup of wine to symbolize a need and desire to share in the spirit and the mystery of the creative process. Next, the couple say their vows. After the vows have been spoken, the groom places a plain gold ring on the bride's finger (fourth finger of the right hand) and says in Hebrew, "Behold, thou art betrothed to me with this ring, according to the rites of Moses and Israel." The *Ketubah* (marriage contract), written in Aramaic, is read aloud by the rabbi, after which the Reader takes another glass of wine, pronounces a blessing, and hands the wine to the groom and bride who taste it.

All Jewish ceremonies end with the traditional *Sheva Berakhot* (seven benedictions), an address by the rabbi, the pronouncement, and the closing benediction. The crushing of a wine glass beneath the groom's heel takes place at the conclusion of the service. At that time, the guests shout out *"Mazel Tov"* as best wishes for the couple.

◆ Orthodox and Conservative

Prior to the wedding, the groom is invited to recite the blessings for the reading of the Torah at a Sabbath service and a *Mi Sheberach* (special prayer) is offered for both the bride and the groom.

Within four days of the wedding, the bride cleanses herself in specially prepared water placed in a *mikveh* (ritual bath).

Orthodox and Conservative practice combine *Erusin* (engagement) and *Nisu'in* (ceremonies) into one service.

When the bride reaches the canopy, she circles the groom seven times (some rabbis reduce the number to three times).

All men must cover their heads with either *yarmulkes* or silk top hats. The groom may wear a *kittel*, or white robe.

The procession usually includes the groom and both sets of parents in recognition of the role played by both parents in raising their child.

The bride's ring is placed upon her right index finger, then the rabbi reads the *ketubah*.

The text of the Conservative *ketubah* is similar to that of the Orthodox *ketubah*, except that the Conservative version contains additional lines that include conditions in the event that the marriage fails and divorce is sought under civil law.

The question of performing interfaith marriages is not open to discussion among Orthodox and Conservative rabbis. They generally adhere strictly to tradition and refuse to officiate at an interfaith marriage. Orthodox rabbis do not recognize any divorces except those granted by *get* (religious (decree).

✦ *Reform*

The processional, altar procedures, and recessional may be similar to those in Christian services. There may be a double-ring ceremony, and the ceremony may not be performed under a *chuppah*. The bride's ring is placed upon her left ring finger. The *ketubah* is omitted.

Rabbis are split on officiating at an interfaith marriage. While the Central Conference of American Rabbis has passed a resolution strongly opposing rabbis officiating at interfaith marriages, they respect the right of every rabbi to make that decision.

Rabbis recognize civil divorces.

Muslim (Islam)

There is no definite religious ceremony of marriage prescribed in the Holy Qur'an. Marriage is not a formal religious act but a legal contract. The ceremony depends upon local customs within the framework of Islam. Islam does not prohibit any local customs as long as they do not conflict with basic Islamic beliefs. The marriage ceremony should preferably take place in a mosque but can take place elsewhere.

Islamic marriage is a serious, mutual commitment of two people before Allah (God) as their witness to achieve the following objectives: mutual love and kindness; truthfulness and straightforwardness; consideration of marriage as the most intimate relationship; realization that perfection only belongs to Allah and an appreciation/tolerance of human shortcomings; mutual respect; being complimentary of each other in front of others; mutual protection of the interests of each other; faithfulness and loyalty to each other; raising children physically, mentally, and spiritually; acting righteously as long-term planning into the everlasting life.

The main purposes of Islamic marriage are: pleasure to Allah; physical, mental, and spiritual peace and tranquility; continuation of the human race; and permanent, healthy, and holy companionship.

The family of the prospective groom sends word of their son's marriage intentions to the father of the prospective bride and requests a visit. During the visit, the family of the prospective groom reads a formal statement of intent (a request to marry the daughter). The bride's family acknowledges the request and indicates whether they accept it. If it is accepted, gifts are presented to the intended bride.

According to Islam, both the husband and wife are allowed to choose their spouse, but the advice of parents and elders is recommended. The marrying couple is allowed to see each other and discuss mutual concerns in the presence of other family members, but Islamic law prohibits them from being alone before the marriage, even after the engagement.

There are three major ceremonies associated with an Islamic marriage:

The *khitbah* (engagement), which is the official announcement of the two persons intending to marry. The marriage cannot take place without the consent and approval of the woman's father or guardian.

The *nikaah, zawaaj* (marriage), which is the public signing of the marriage contract. A *qadi* (or *ma'dhun*, in Arab countries) delivers a sermon containing information from the Holy Qur'an in Arabic and explains it in English. Then, an oral consent by the bride and acceptance by the groom of the contract takes place in the presence of at least two witnesses. At that time, the couple is bound to each other by canonical law. The actual ceremony may vary according to the discretion of the qadi. The bride's family will often provide food and special sweets for the guests after the ceremony.

The *valimah* (post consummation) takes place the next day or as soon as possible. It is the responsibility of the groom and his family to provide a feast according to their financial status.

Since both Christians and Jews believe in Moses and Christians believe in Jesus, and both Moses and Jesus are prophets of Islam, a Muslim man is permitted to marry a

Christian or Jewish woman. However, they are not allowed to marry women from nonmonotheistic religions. On the other hand, a Muslim woman cannot marry a non-Muslim man because the other religions do not believe in Mohammed.

Protestant

Because of the strong Protestant tradition in the United States, the Protestant wedding ceremonies are probably the most familiar. Most of the Protestant wedding services are similar.

The Protestant wedding differs from that of other religions in that it is a worship service where the will of God is thought to be served and the lordship of Jesus is proclaimed.

Although there are no formal prohibitions on performing weddings on certain days, some clergy do not perform weddings on Sundays and religious holidays. Since rules about the use of music vary, prior approval of the clergy to use specific music is recommended.

◆ Episcopal

Episcopal priests will usually not perform weddings during Lent, on solemn holy days such as Christmas or Easter, and on any day of abstinence.

Episcopal canon requires the couple to give notice of their pending wedding at least thirty days before the scheduled date. The bride and groom sign a written Declaration of Intent prior to the service.

Holy Communion is always a part of the service.

An Episcopal priest must receive the consent of the Bishop prior to performing a wedding for a divorced person.

◆ Lutheran

Lutheran ministers will normally not perform weddings on solemn holy days, such as Christmas and Easter, or on any day of abstinence.

The guests at a Lutheran wedding ceremony are considered part of the service.

Religious Society of Friends (Quakers)

Prior approval of the marriage by the Society of Friends is required. The wedding is conducted during the worship meeting and there is no music. The bride is not given away, and a clergy/officiant does not pronounce the couple married. The bride and groom, seated in the front row meeting hall, rise, join hands, and exchange their vows. They sit down, and the marriage certificate is brought to them to be signed. The certificate is then read aloud by a member of the meeting. After the worship meeting is concluded, the couple is ushered out, and each member of the congregation signs the certificate as witnesses. Exchanging rings is not required. No one individual officiates at the service or declares the couple husband and wife. It is the Quaker belief that only God can create a union and give it significance.

Contemporary Quaker services may be similar to other Protestant weddings.

Seventh-day Adventist

If no reception is to follow, the Seventh-day Adventist wedding is considered a religious ceremony and may be held on Saturday, which is the Adventist Sabbath. If the ceremony is followed by a reception, it is viewed as secular and cannot be held on the Sabbath. In that case, the ceremony is normally held on Sunday.

The North American Seventh-day Adventist service usually does not include the exchange of rings since jewelry is considered worldly and is thus against their beliefs.

Unitarian

The Unitarian Church does not use a standard service. Each minister is allowed to compose the service to reflect the individuality of each wedding couple.

❏ Symbolism

Breaking of a glass (Jewish) — A Jewish wedding tradition where, at the end of the ceremony, the groom wraps a glass in cloth, places it on the ground, and steps on it. This is a reminder of the destruction of the holy temple in Jerusalem.

Bridal bouquet — Flowers symbolize fidelity, love, fulfillment, and happiness.

Canopy — For Jews, the canopy symbolizes the ancient bridal chamber of consummation, shelter from the open sky in ancient times, and the home that the couple will live in.

Crowns (Eastern Orthodox) — The crowns of martyrdom, since every true marriage involves immeasurable mutual sacrifice.

Cup of wine (Eastern Orthodox) — The cup of life. The common cup signifies living in accord and mutual understanding with one another, sharing equally the cup of joy and sorrow.

Diamond — A medieval symbol of durability and enduring love.

Engagement ring — In 1215, Pope Innocent III declared that weddings must be held in the church. In addition, he decreed a waiting period between betrothal and the wedding. The engagement ring became a way of indicating that the woman was spoken for.

Guests — Family and friends invited to receive the news, witness the wedding ceremony, and celebrate the union.

Lucky penny in your shoe (English) — A new penny is worn in the heel of the bride's left shoe to guarantee wealth and prosperity in the future.

Procession — The bringing of the bride to the groom.

Ring — A binding of the marriage commitment; unending love; and, when gold, lasting beauty and purity. In the past, the groom was expected to deliver to the bride an object of worth, representing his barter price for her. This custom has evolved into the modern-day wedding ring.

Something old (English) — An article that has belonged to a happily married woman to transfer happiness to the new bride.

Something new (English) — An article (such as the wedding dress) to symbolize both the beauty of the new relationship and prosperity.

Something borrowed (English) — An article, usually made of gold, to guarantee wealth and good fortune in the future.

Something blue (Jewish) — An article (such as a ribbon) to symbolize fidelity, modesty, and love.

Vows — Public pronouncements of the bride and groom. Promises expressing deep and personal commitment that the bride and groom make to each other and their family and friends.

Wedding — Formal announcement and expression of the bonds of love between a couple. Also, the formal expression of consent to the marriage by the bride's parents.

Wedding day fasting (Jewish) — For Jews, this is a fast from sunrise on the wedding day until the wedding meal, serving as a symbol of sacrifice, atonement, and a cleansing of the self of all sins prior to marriage.

White bridal gown—From ancient times, white was the symbol of joy and celebration. Only since the early twentieth century has the color represented purity. During recent times, the original meaning has been returning.

Wine—From the wedding in Cana, Galilee, where water was turned into wine by Jesus. For Jews, wine is a symbol of sanctification.

Unity candle—The side candles represent the couple's individual, separate, distinct lives up to the wedding ceremony. These two candles are merged to light the larger center candle to express the couple's union in Christ. The side candles stay lit to symbolize that their individual personalities remain within the marriage relationship.

TABLE 12-1

Sample Order of Wedding Ceremony

Catholic (Roman)
Entrance (Processional)
Greeting
Opening prayer
Old Testament reading
Responsory Psalm
New Testament reading
Alleluia
Gospel reading
Homily (Sermon)
Rite of marriage
    Consent
    Vows
    Ring exchange
    Prayer of the faithful
Liturgy of the Eucharist
Lord's Prayer
Nuptial blessing
Sign of peace
Communion
Solemn blessing
Dismissal
Recessional

Eastern Rite (Orthodox)
Betrothal service
    Intent
    Question
Processional
The rings
Sacrament of holy matrimony
    The crowning
    The Epistle
    The Gospel
    The common cup
    The bridal procession
Words of exhortation
Prayer
Benediction
Recessional

Hindu
Worship of fire god — Agni
Gift exchange
Circling the fire god (seven times)
    Repeating a different vow each
    time

Jewish*
Processional
    Introductory blessing
    Prayer
    Cup of wine
Marriage Service
    Vows
    Bride's ring
    Ketubah
    Groom's ring (optional)
    Blessing
    Cup of wine
    Homily (Sermon)
    Pronouncement
Benediction
Break glass
Recessional

There are variations among the Orthodox, Conservative, and Reform wedding services.

Muslim
Opening prayer
Signing of the marriage contract
Sermon (Arabic and English)
Oral consent of the bride
Oral acceptance of the groom

Protestant**
Processional
Invocation/words of welcome
Prayer
Address/sermon
Giving of the Bride/blessing of the
    marriage
Charge/challenge
Betrothal pledge
Exchange of marriage vows
Ring exchange
Pronouncement
Prayer and Lord's Prayer
Communion (optional)
Benediction
Announcement
Recessional

**There are many variations among the denominations*

137

CHAPTER 13

How Can We Personalize Our Ceremony?

Your wedding ceremony can be highly distinctive and individualized if you use your imagination to personalize your expression of love and commitment.

The practice of writing your own vows and/or selecting personally meaningful readings is fitting. It demonstrates to your family and friends that you are aware of the significance of your relationship, are able to express your feelings, and want to make the ceremony a memorable, intimate, personal celebration.

Your vows are the focal point of the deep, personal commitment you are both making. Vows are the public pronouncements in which you express your deepest feelings and intentions. Vows make public the promises you are making to each other for your lifetime together. Vows convey the aura and tone of your ceremony.

Writing your own vows can add a personal touch, depth, warmth, and freshness to your ceremony. A few well-chosen phrases can convey a wealth of thoughts and feelings. The vows you write and/or readings you select can express the values by which you both want to conduct your married life.

You may also include appropriate religious and/or secular reading(s) which express your feelings toward each other, your concept of married life, and/or your religious heritage. A brief reading may convey special thoughts that you wish to share with each other and your guests. You may select Bible passages, poems, and/or literary works with good effect. You should choose readings which have the most significance to you, make you feel comfortable, and express the theme of the wedding ceremony.

When writing your vows and/or making your reading selections, you should talk to each other, resolve any differing preferences, and keep an open mind. You should also confer with the clergy/officiant who will be conducting your ceremony for assistance and concurrence.

❏ Vows

If you accept the challenge of writing your own vows, this section provides you with some samples to browse through. You can select, adapt, mix, discard, and/or use these vows as guides to help you compose the vows which contain the unique expression of your feelings. Further samples and information may be found in *Wedding Vows* by Peg Kehret, copyright © 1989 by Meriwether Publishing Ltd., P.O. Box 7710, Colorado Springs, CO 80933.

Bahai

* "We will all, verily, abide by the Will of God."

Catholic (Roman)

* I, (name), take you, (name), to be my wife/husband. I promise to be true to you in good times and in bad, in sickness and in health. I will love and honor you all the days of my life.

* I, (name), take you, (name), for my lawful wife/husband, to have and to hold, from this day forward, for better, for worse, for richer, for poorer, in sickness and in health, until death do us part.

Contemporary

* I (name), take you, (name), to be my wife/husband, according to the ordinances of God, to love and cherish as long as we both shall live.

* (Groom's/Bride's name), I promise with God's help to be your faithful wife/husband, to love and serve you as

Christ commands, as long as we both shall live.

- I, (name), take you, (name), to be my wife/husband, to live with you, care for you, and to love you alone for as long as I live. I promise to be understanding, forgiving, and seeking your happiness as we grow together in God's grace.

- I, (name), take you, (name), to be my wedded wife/husband, to have and to hold from this day, to care for and to encourage in both good times and bad. I promise to live for Christ and with you in the full awareness of trust and love, and with this commitment, I pledge to you my love.

- I, (name), take you, (name), as my lawful wife/ husband, to walk beside me when things are good and when things are bad. I pledge to you my undying love and constant faithfulness. All I have or hope to have, I give to you as my life partner. I pledge to you my help, my support, my love, and my prayers. I pledge to remain faithfully yours until death separates us. I ask God's help in keeping this solemn vow.

- I, (name), take you, (name), to be my cherished wife/husband. I promise with all my heart to walk beside you in days of adversity and in days of great happiness, to provide a shoulder to cry on, and a heart that understands. I will rejoice with you, I will weep with you, I will create life with you in reverence. I commit my love to you. I will grow with you in trust, share my possessions, and communicate openly and honestly with you. I will be faithful to you and you alone until Christ calls me home, and I will seek to create a marriage where you can find refuge from fear, and strength in a troubled world.

- I, (name), take you, (name), to be my wedded wife/husband. I give to you the love in my heart, the hope in my soul, the faith of my spirit. I promise full, joyful cooperation in building a Christian home. I will

141

support you in your aspirations, pray with you in your trials, share your burdens, and labor with you to make our marriage a joy. I will live close to my God, so you may trust me at all times. I will laugh with you in the happy times, comfort you in the sad times, and create life with you. With you, I will honor our God and his Son, Jesus Christ, all of our days.

- I, (name), take you, (name), to be my wedded wife/husband, to have and to hold from this day forward. In times of plenty or in times of poverty, in health and sickness, I will love you. I will cherish each meaningful day that God unfolds to us, depending on his provision and grace. I will celebrate the joyous moments with you, and weep with you in sorrow and trouble. I will be faithful to you and to you alone till in death do we part.

- I, (name), offer myself completely to you, (name), to be your husband/wife in marriage. I promise to love you with all of my heart, and to be true, faithful, patient, kind, and unselfish in this love. I promise to stand beside you always, in times of joy, in times of trial, and in times of sorrow. I dedicate our marriage and our home to God. I pledge myself and all that I am to you in love.

- I, (name), take you, (name), as my wedded wife/husband. Though the unknown future brings joy or sorrow, health or sickness, prosperity or adversity, sunshine or shadow, hopes fulfilled or dreams shattered, I pledge to be true to you for the rest of my life.

- I, (name), having full confidence that our abiding faith in each other as human beings will last our lifetime, take you, (name), to be my wedded husband/wife. I promise to be your loving and faithful husband/wife in prosperity and in need, in joy and in sorrow, in sickness and in health, and to respect your privileges as an individual as long as we both shall live.

- (Bride's/Groom's name), I love you as Christ loves us,

142

unconditionally, unselfishly, and eternally. I receive you as my wife/husband, my helpmate, a gift from God. I promise to honor, cherish, respect, and trust you. I promise to work beside you to build a loving and a happy home. I commit myself to do these things through the power of the Holy Spirit for all of my life.

♦ I, (name), take you, (name), to be my wife/husband in Christian marriage. I promise God and I promise you that I will love and cherish you. I will provide a shoulder to cry on, a heart that understands, a warm and happy home to live in, and open arms to hold you. I will be faithful to you and to you alone. I will pray for you, I will weep with you in sorrow, rejoice with you in blessings, and be your faithful companion until God calls us home. I make this vow to you, so help me God.

♦ I, (name), receive you, (name), to be my wedded wife/husband. I accept you as a precious gift from God. I love you with a love only Christ himself could place within my heart. I promise to give myself to you as Christ gave himself to the church. I wish to have and to hold you from this day forward, for better, for worse, for richer, for poorer, in sickness and in health, to love and to cherish as long as we both shall live, according to God's holy ordinance.

♦ I accept you, (name), as a person, and as my wife/husband, with your strengths and with your weaknesses. I promise to be loyal to you in health or illness, to share what I have and who I am, to love enough to risk being hurt, to trust when I misunderstand, to weep with you in sorrow, to celebrate with you in joy, and to live with you in reverence.

Jewish (Reform)

♦ Yes, I, (name), choose you, (name), to be my wife/husband, my friend, my love, the mother/father of our children. I will be yours in plenty and in want, in sickness and in health, in failure and in triumph. I will cherish you and respect you, comfort and encourage you, and together we shall live, freed and bound by our love.

Muslim (Islam)

+ Bride: I pledge, in honesty and with sincerity, to be for you an obedient and faithful wife.

   Groom: I pledge, in honesty and with sincerity, to be for you a faithful and helpful husband.

Protestant

+ In the name of God, I, (name), take you, (name), to be my wife/husband, to have and to hold from this day forward, for better, for worse, for richer, for poorer, in sickness and in health, to love and to cherish, until we are parted by death. This is my solemn vow. (Episcopal)

+ I, (name), take thee, (name), to be my wedded wife/husband, to have and to hold from this day forward, for better, for worse, for richer, for poorer, in sickness and in health, to love and to cherish, till death us do part, according to God's holy ordinance; and thereto I plight/give thee my troth. (Episcopal)

+ I take you, (name), to be my wife/husband from this day forward, to join with you and share all that is to come, and I promise to be faithful to you until death departs us. (Lutheran)

+ In the name of God, I, (name), take you, (name), to be my wife/husband, to have and to hold from this day forward, for better, for worse, for richer, for poorer, in sickness and in health, to love and to cherish until we are parted by death. This is my solemn vow. (Methodist)

+ I, (name), take you to be my wedded wife/husband, and I do promise and covenant, before God and these witnesses, to be your loving and faithful wife/husband, in plenty and in want, in joy and in sorrow, in sickness and in health, as long as we both shall live.

(Presbyterian)

- In the presence of God and these our friends, I take thee, (name), to be my wife/husband, promising with divine assistance to be unto thee a loving and faithful wife/husband as long as we both shall live. (Quaker)

Remarriage

- I, (name), promise you, (name), to be your husband/wife as long as I live. I promise to love you and to support your growing toward full maturity. I promise to seek peace for ourselves, for our children, and for the world which encircles us. As I commit myself to care for you, I also offer myself into your loving care, now and throughout our lives.

- Because you have brought so much joy into my life and taught me the healing power of love, have shown me how to trust and feel and give the best that is in me freely and fearlessly, I pledge to you my unswerving devotion and the love which will be yours for as long as I live.

- I bring with me all of my yesterdays, but also the promise of all of my tomorrows. Let me touch your life with mine — but let me not stand in your shadow. Let me blend all that is me with all that is you so that we can bring new growth to one another. I promise in the midst of our families and friends that I will love and cherish you and will be faithful to you alone as long as I live.

Renewal of Vows

- Blessed with you, (name), I give thanks to God for our togetherness through all these years which has enriched our lives beyond measure, and promise again with all my heart to love you and to cherish you all the days of our lives.

- (Number of years) years ago, I pledged my loyalty to you, (name), as your wedded husband/wife, to live together after God's ordinance, in the holy estate of

145

matrimony. I promised to love you, comfort you, honor and keep you, in sickness and in health. I further promised that, forsaking all others, I would keep myself only unto you, so long as we both shall live. During these (number of years) years, I have been faithful to that pledge. Now, again, at the beginning of the (number of year) year of our life together, in the presence of God, in the presence of our family, and in the presence of friends who have gathered for this happy occasion, I renew these vows, pledging myself to continue my devotion to you as long as we both shall live.

Traditional

* I, (name), take thee, (name), to be my wedded wife/husband, to have and to hold from this day forward, for better, for worse, for richer, for poorer, in sickness and in health, to love and to cherish till death us do part, according to God's holy ordinance; and thereto I pledge thee my faith.

* I, (name), take you, (name), to be my wife/husband, to have and to hold from this day forward, for better, for worse, for richer, for poorer, in sickness and in health, to love and to cherish, till death do us part. This is my solemn vow according to God's holy ordinance; and thereto I plight you my troth.

Unitarian

* I, (name), take you, (name), to be my wife/husband, to have and to hold from this day forward, for better, for worse, for richer, for poorer, in sickness and in health, to love and cherish always.

❒ Readings

The readings which you select not only enrich your wedding ceremony, but can also deepen the spiritual meaning. Blending in readings which you have chosen because of their significance to your unique relationship adds a meaningful, personal dimension to the ceremony.

Since selecting readings is very much a personal matter, there is a limitless source of potential readings. This section only provides some possible sources for passages; you may already have favorites of your own.

The readings which you select may be read by the clergy/officiant, by a member of the wedding party, by a member of your family, or by special friends.

Religious

♦ *Holy Bible* (Eastern Orthodox, Protestant, Roman Catholic)

See your clergy to determine which translations of the Bible are acceptable. The following Old and New Testament verses are from The New King James Version. Copyright © 1979, 1980, 1982, Thomas Nelson, Inc. The selections from the Apocrypha verses are taken from the *New American Bible*, copyright © 1970, Confraternity of Christian Doctrine, Washington, DC.

📖 Old Testament

📃 Genesis 1:26-31 (Creation of Man and Woman)

Then God said, "Let us make man in our image, according to our likeness; let them have dominion over the fish of the sea, over the birds of the air, and over the cattle, over all the earth and over every creeping thing that creeps on the earth." So God created man in his own image; in the image of God he created him; male and female he created them. Then God blessed them, and God said to them, "Be fruitful and multiply; fill the earth and subdue it; have dominion over the fish of the sea, over the birds of the air, and over every living thing that moves on the earth." And God said, "See, I have given you every herb that yields seeds which is on the face of all the earth, and every tree whose fruit yields seed; to you it shall be for food. Also, to every beast of the earth, to every bird of the air, and to everything that creeps on the earth, in which there is life, I have given every green herb for food"; and it was so. Then God saw everything

147

that he had made, and indeed it was very good. So the evening and the morning were the sixth day.

📖 Genesis 2:18-25 (Marriage Instituted by God)*

And the Lord God said, "It is not good that man should be alone; I will make him a helper comparable to him." Out of the ground the Lord God formed every beast of the field and every bird of the air, and brought them to Adam to see what he would call them. And whatever Adam called each living creature, that was its name. So Adam gave names to all cattle, to the birds of the air, and to every beast of the field. But for Adam there was not found a helper comparable to him. And the Lord God caused a deep sleep to fall on Adam, and he slept; and he took one of his ribs, and closed up the flesh in its place. Then the rib which the Lord God had taken from man he made into a woman, and he brought her to the man. And Adam said: "This is now bone of my bones and flesh of my flesh; she shall be called woman, because she was taken out of man." Therefore a man shall leave his father and mother and be joined to his wife, and they shall become one flesh. And they were both naked, the man and his wife, and were not ashamed.

📖 Genesis 24:48-51, 58-67 (Isaac's Marriage)*

"And I bowed my head and worshipped the Lord, and blessed the Lord God of my master Abraham, who had led me in the way of truth to take the daughter of my master's brother for his son." "Now if you will deal kindly and truly with my master, tell me. And if not, tell me, that I may turn to the right hand or to the left." Then Laban and Bethuel answered and said, "The thing comes from the Lord; we cannot speak to you either bad or good." "Here is Rebekah before you; take her and go, and let her be your master's son's wife, as the Lord has spoken."... Then they called Rebekah and said to her, "Will you go with this man?" And she said, "I will go." So they sent away Rebekah their sister and her nurse, and Abraham's servant and his men. And they blessed

Rebekah and said to her: "Our sister, may you become the mother of thousands of tens thousands; and may your descendants possess the gates of those who hate them."

Then Rebekah and her maids arose, and they rode on the camels and followed the man. So the servant took Rebekah and departed. Now Isaac came from the way of Beer Lahai Roi, for he dwelt in the South. And Isaac went out to meditate in the field in the evening; and he lifted his eyes and looked, and there, the camels were coming. Then Rebekah lifted her eyes, and when she saw Isaac she dismounted from her camel; for she had said to the servant, "Who is this man walking in the field to meet us?" And the servant said, "It is my master." So she took a veil and covered herself.

And the servant told Isaac all the things that he had done. Then Isaac brought her into his mother Sarah's tent; and he took Rebekah and she became his wife, and he loved her. So Isaac was comforted after his mother's death.

📄 Ruth 1:16 (Ruth's Love Demonstrated)*

But Ruth said: "Entreat me not to leave you, or to turn back from following after you; for wherever you go, I will go; and wherever you lodge, I will lodge; Your people shall be my people, and your God, my God."

📄 Psalm 67 (God Shall Govern the Earth)*

God be merciful to us and bless us, and cause his face to shine upon us; Selah. That your way may be known on earth, your salvation among all nations. Let the peoples praise you, O God; let all the peoples praise you. Oh, let the nations be glad and sing for joy! For you shall judge the people righteously, and govern the nations on earth; Selah. Let the peoples praise you, O God; let all the peoples praise you. Then the earth shall yield her increase; God, our own God, shall bless us. God shall bless us, and all the ends of the earth shall fear him.

📑 Psalm 112:1-8 (Blessing of Those Who Fear God)*

Praise the Lord! Blessed is the man who fears the Lord, who delights greatly in his commandments. His descendants will be mighty on earth; the generation of the upright will be blessed. Wealth and riches will be in his house, and his righteousness endures forever. Unto the upright there arises light in the darkness; He is gracious, and full of compassion, and righteous. A good man deals graciously and lends; he will guide his affairs with discretion. Surely he will never be shaken; the righteous will be in everlasting remembrance. He will not be afraid of evil tidings; his heart is steadfast, trusting in the Lord. His heart is established; he will not be afraid, until he sees his desire upon his enemies.

📑 Psalm 127 (Children Are God's Heritage)*

Unless the Lord builds the house, they labor in vain who build it; unless the Lord guards the city, the watchman stays awake in vain. It is vain for you to rise up early, to sit up late, to eat the bread of sorrows; for so he gives his beloved sleep. Behold, children are a heritage from the Lord, the fruit of the womb is his reward. Like arrows in the hand of a warrior, so are the children of one's youth. Happy is the man who has his quiver full of them; they shall not be ashamed, but shall speak with their enemies in the gate.

📑 Psalm 128 (Blessing on the House of the God-Fearing)*

Blessed is every one who fears the Lord, who walks in his ways. When you eat the labor of your hands, you shall be happy, and it shall be well with you. Your wife shall be like a fruitful vine in the very heart of your house, your children like olive plants all around your table. Behold, thus shall the man be blessed who fears the Lord. The Lord bless you out of Zion, and may you see the good of Jerusalem all the days of your life. Yes, may you see your children's children.

*From The New King James Version. Copyright © 1979, 1980, 1982, Thomas Nelson, Inc.

📃 Psalm 134 (Praise the Lord)*

Behold, bless the Lord, all you servants of the Lord, who by night stand in the house of the Lord! Lift up your hands in the sanctuary, and bless the Lord. The Lord who made heaven and earth bless you from Zion!

📃 Proverbs 24:3-4 (A House Is Built)*

Through wisdom a house is built, and by understanding it is established; by knowledge the rooms are filled with all precious and pleasant riches.

📃 Proverbs 31:10-12 (Wise Woman)*

Who can find a virtuous wife? For her worth is far above rubies. The heart of her husband safely trusts her; so he will have no lack of gain. She does him good and not evil all the days of her life.

📃 Song of Solomon (Songs) 2:8-10, 14 (Visit of King to Bride's Home)*

The voice of my beloved! Behold, he comes leaping upon the mountains, skipping upon the hills. My beloved is like a gazelle or a young stag. Behold, he stands behind our wall; he is looking through the windows, gazing through the lattice. My beloved spoke, and said to me: "Rise up, my love, my fair one, and come away..." "O my dove, in the clefts of the rock, in the secret places of the cliff, let me see your countenance, let me hear your voice; for your voice is sweet, and your countenance is lovely."

📃 Song of Solomon (Songs) 7:10-12 (Growing in Love)*

I am my beloved's, and his desire is toward me. Come, my beloved, let us go forth to the field; let us lodge in the villages. Let us get up early to the vineyards; let us see if the vine has budded, whether the grape blossoms are open, and the pomegranates are in bloom. There I will give you my love.

---

*From The New King James Version. Copyright © 1979, 1980, 1982, Thomas Nelson, Inc.

📜 Song of Solomon (Songs) 8:6-7
(Love Is as Strong as Death)*

Set me as a seal upon your heart, as seal upon your arm; for love is as strong as death, jealousy as cruel as the grave; its flames are flames of fire, a most vehement flame. Many waters cannot quench love, nor can the floods drown it. If a man would give for love all the wealth of his house, it would be utterly despised.

📜 Jeremiah 31:31-34 (The New Covanant)*

"Behold, the days are coming," says the Lord, "when I will make a new covenant with the house of Israel and with the house of Judah, not according to the covenant that I made with their fathers in the day that I took them by the hand to bring them out of the land of Egypt, my covenant which they broke, though I was a husband to them", says the Lord. "But this is the covenant that I will make with the house of Israel: After those days," says the Lord, "I will put my law in their minds, and write it on their hearts; and I will be their God, and they shall be my people. No more shall every man teach his neighbor, and every man his brother, saying, 'Know the Lord,' for they shall know me, from the least of them to the greatest of them," says the Lord. "For I will forgive their iniquity, and their sin I will remember no more."

📖 *New Testament*

📜 Matthew 5:2-12 (The Beatitudes)*

Then he opened his mouth and taught them, saying: "Blessed are the poor in spirit, for theirs is the kingdom of heaven. Blessed are those who mourn, for they shall be comforted. Blessed are the meek, for they shall inherit the earth. Blessed are those who hunger and thirst for righteousness, for they shall be filled. Blessed are the merciful, for they shall obtain mercy. Blessed are the pure in heart, for they shall see God. Blessed are the peacemakers, for they shall be called sons of God. Blessed are those who are persecuted for righteousness' sake, for theirs is the kingdom of heaven. Blessed are you when they revile and persecute you, and say all kinds of evil against you falsely for my sake. Rejoice and be exceedingly glad, for great is your reward in heaven, for so they persecuted the prophets who were before you."

📑 Matthew 7:21, 24-27 (House Built on Rock)*

"Not everyone who says to me, 'Lord, Lord,' shall enter the kingdom of heaven, but he who does the will of my Father in heaven. Therefore whoever hears these sayings of mine, and does them, I will liken him to a wise man who built his house on the rock: and the rain descended, the floods came, and the winds blew and beat on that house; and it did not fall, for it was founded on the rock. Now everyone who hears these sayings of mine, and does not do them, will be like a foolish man who built his house on the sand: and the rain descended, the floods came, and the winds blew and beat on that house; and it fell. And great was its fall."

📑 Matthew 19:4-6 (Indissolubility of Marriage)*

And he answered and said to them, "Have you not read that he who made them at the beginning 'made them male and female,' and said, 'For this reason a man shall leave his father and mother and be joined to his wife, and the two shall become one flesh'? So then, they are no longer two but one flesh. Therefore what God has joined together, let not man separate."

📑 Matthew 22:35-40 (Greatest Commandment)*

Then one of them, a lawyer, asked him a question, testing him, and saying, "Teacher, which is the great commandment in the law?" Jesus said to him, "'You shall love the Lord your God with all your heart, with all your soul, and with all your mind.' This is the first and great commandment. And the second is like it: 'You shall love your neighbor as yourself.' On these two commandments hang all the Law and the Prophets."

*From The New King James Version. Copyright © 1979, 1980, 1982, Thomas Nelson, Inc.

153

📖 Mark 10:6-9 (What God Has Joined)*

"But from the beginning of the creation, God 'made them male and female.' 'For this reason a man shall leave his father and mother and be joined to his wife, and the two shall become one flesh'; so then they are no longer two, but one flesh. Therefore what God has joined together, let not man separate."

📖 John 2:1-11 (Wedding in Cana)*

On the third day there was a wedding in Cana of Galilee, and the mother of Jesus was there. Now both Jesus and his disciples were invited to the wedding. And when they ran out of wine, the mother of Jesus said to him, "They have no wine." Jesus said to her, "Woman, what does your concern have to do with me? My hour has not yet come." His mother said to the servants, "Whatever he says to you, do it." Now there were set there six waterpots of stone, according to the manner of purification of the Jews, containing twenty or thirty gallons apiece. Jesus said to them, "Fill the waterpots with water." And they filled them up to the brim. And he said to them, "Draw some out now, and take it to the master of the feast." And they took it. When the master of the feast had tasted the water that was made wine, and did not know where it came from (but the servants who had drawn the water knew), the master of the feast called the bridegroom. And he said to him, "Every man at the beginning sets out the good wine, and when the guests have drunk, then that which is inferior; but you have kept the good wine until now." This beginning of signs Jesus did in Cana of Galilee, and manifested his glory; and his disciples believed in him.

📖 John 15:9-12 (Abide in My Love)*

"As the Father loved me, I also have loved you; abide in my love. If you keep my commandments, you will abide in my love, just as I have kept my Father's commandments and abide in his love. These things I have spoken to you, that my joy may remain in you, and that your joy may be full. This is my commandment, that you love one another as I have loved you."

*From The New King James Version. Copyright © 1979, 1980, 1982, Thomas Nelson, Inc.

📑 John 17:20-26 (Christ Prays for All Believers)*

"I do not pray for these alone, but also for those who will believe in me through their word; that they all may be one, as you, Father, are in me, and I in you; that they also may be one in us, that the world may believe that you sent me. And the glory which you gave me I have given them, that they may be one just as we are one: I in them, and you in me; that they may be made perfect in one, and that the world may know that you have sent me, and have loved them as you have loved me. Father, I desire that they also whom you gave me may be with me where I am, that they may behold my glory which you have given me; for you loved me before the foundation of the world. O righteous Father! The world has not known you, but I have known you; and these have known that you sent me. And I have declared to them your name, and will declare it, that the love with which you loved me may be in them, and I in them."

📑 Romans 8:31-35, 37-39 (The Love of Christ)*

What then shall we say to these things? If God is for us, who can be against us? He who did not spare his own Son, but delivered him up for us all, how shall he not with him also freely give us all things? Who shall bring a charge against God's elect? It is God who justifies. Who is he who condemns? It is Christ who died, and furthermore is also risen, who is even at the right hand of God, who also makes intercessions for us. Who shall separate us from the love of Christ? Shall tribulation, or distress, or persecution, or famine, or nakedness, or peril, or sword?...Yet in all these things we are more than conquerors through him who loved us. For I am persuaded that neither death nor life, nor angels nor principalities nor powers, nor things present nor things to come, nor height, nor depth, nor any other created thing, shall be able to separate us from the love of God which is in Christ Jesus our Lord.

---

*From The New King James Version. Copyright © 1979, 1980, 1982, Thomas Nelson, Inc.

🔲 Romans 12:1-2, 9-12 (Responsibilities Toward God)*

I beseech you therefore, brethren, by the mercies of God, that you present your bodies a living sacrifice, holy, acceptable to God, which is your reasonable service. And do not be conformed to this world, but be transformed by the renewing of your mind, that you may prove what is that good and acceptable and perfect will of God...Let love be without hypocrisy. Abhor what is evil. Cling to what is good. Be kindly affectionate to one another with brotherly love, in honor giving preference to one another; not lagging in diligence, fervent in spirit, serving the Lord; rejoicing in hope, patient in tribulation, continuing steadfastly in prayer.

🔲 1 Corinthians 6:13-15, 17-20
(One Spirit With Him)*

Foods for the stomach and the stomach for foods, but God will destroy both it and them. Now the body is not for sexual immorality but for the Lord, and the Lord for the body. And God both raised up the Lord and will also raise us up by his power. Do you not know that your bodies are members of Christ? Shall I then take the members of Christ and make them members of a harlot? Certainly not!...But he who is joined to the Lord is one spirit with him. Flee sexual immorality. Every sin that a man does is outside the body, but he who commits sexual immorality sins against his own body. Or do you not know that your body is the temple of the Holy Spirit who is in you, whom you have from God, and you are not your own? For you were bought at a price; therefore glorify God in your body and in your spirit, which are God's.

🔲 1 Corinthians 13:1-8, 13 (The Love Chapter)*

Though I speak with the tongues of men and of angels, but have not love, I have become as sounding brass or a clanging cymbal. And though I have the gift of prophecy, and understand all mysteries and all knowledge, and though I have all faith, so that I could remove mountains, but have not love, I am nothing. And though I bestow all my goods to feed

*From The New King James Version. Copyright © 1979, 1980, 1982, Thomas Nelson, Inc.

the poor, and though I give my body to be burned, but have not love, it profits me nothing. Love suffers long and is kind; love does not envy; love does not parade itself, is not puffed up; does not behave rudely, does not seek its own, is not provoked, thinks no evil; does not rejoice in iniquity, but rejoices in the truth; bears all things, believes all things, hopes all things, endures all things. Love never fails...And now abide faith, hope, love, these three; but the greatest of these is love.

📖 Ephesians 3:14-21 (The Love of Christ)*

For this reason I bow my knees to the Father of our Lord Jesus Christ, from whom the whole family in heaven and earth is named, that he would grant you, according to the riches of his glory, to be strengthened with might through his Spirit in the inner man, that Christ may dwell in your hearts through faith; that you, being rooted and grounded in love, may be able to comprehend with all the saints what is the width and length and depth and height to know the love of Christ which passes knowledge; that you may be filled with all the fullness of God. Now to him who is able to do exceedingly abundantly above all that we ask or think, according to the power that works in us, to him be glory in the church by Christ Jesus throughout all ages, world without end. Amen.

📖 Ephesians 5:20-33 (Mystery of Marriage)*

Giving thanks always for all things to God the Father in the name of our Lord Jesus Christ, submitting to one another in the fear of God. Wives, submit to your own husbands, as to the Lord. For the husband is head of the wife, as also Christ is head of the church; and he is the Savior of the body. Therefore, just as the church is subject to Christ, so let the wives be to their own husbands in everything. Husbands, love your wives, just as Christ also loved the church and gave himself for it, that he might sanctify and cleanse it with the washing of water by the word, that he might present it to himself a glorious church, not having spot or wrinkle or any such thing, but that it should be holy and without blemish. So

*From The New King James Version. Copyright © 1979, 1980, 1982, Thomas Nelson, Inc.

husbands ought to love their own wives as their own bodies; he who loves his wife loves himself. For no one ever hated his own flesh, but nourishes and cherishes it, just as the Lord does the church. For we are members of his body, of his flesh and of his bones. "For this reason a man shall leave his father and mother and be joined to his wife, and the two shall become one flesh." This is a great mystery, but I speak concerning Christ and the church. Nevertheless let each one of you in particular so love his own wife as himself, and let the wife see that she respects her husband.

📖 Colossians 3:12-17 (Love and Thanksgiving)*

Therefore, as the elect of God, holy and beloved, put on tender mercies, kindness, humbleness of mind, meekness, long-suffering; bearing with one another, and forgiving one another, if anyone has a complaint against another, even as Christ forgave you, so you also must do. But above all these things put on love, which is the bond of perfection. And let the peace of God rule in your hearts, to which also you were called in one body; and be thankful. Let the word of Christ dwell in you richly in all wisdom, teaching and admonishing one another in psalms and hymns and spiritual songs, singing with grace in your hearts to the Lord. And whatever you do in word or deed, do all in the name of the Lord Jesus, giving thanks to God the Father through him.

📖 I Peter 3:1-9 (Submission in Marriage)*

Likewise you wives, be submissive to your own husbands, that even if some do not obey the word, they, without a word, may be won by the conduct of their wives, when they observe your chaste conduct accompanied by fear. Do not let your beauty be that outward adorning of arranging the hair, of wearing gold, or of putting on fine apparel; but let it be the hidden person of the heart, with the incorruptible ornament or a gentle and quiet spirit, which is very precious in the sight of God. For in this manner, in former times, the holy women who trusted in God also adorned themselves, being submis-

*From The New King James Version. Copyright © 1979, 1980, 1982, Thomas Nelson, Inc.

sive to their own husbands, as Sarah obeyed Abraham, calling him lord, whose daughters you are if you do good and are not afraid with any terror. Likewise you husbands, dwell with them with understanding, giving honor to the wife, as to the weaker vessel, and as being heirs together of the grace of life, that your prayers may not be hindered. Finally, all of you be of one mind, having compassion for one another; love as brothers, be tenderhearted, be courteous; not returning evil for evil or reviling for reviling, but on the contrary blessing, knowing that you were called to this, that you may inherit a blessing.

📖 1 John 3:18-24 (Love in Deed and Truth)*

My little children, let us not love in word or in tongue, but in deed and in truth. And by this we know that we are of the truth, and shall assure our hearts before him. For if our heart condemns us, God is greater than our heart, and knows all things. Beloved, if our heart does not condemn us, we have confidence toward God. And whatever we ask we receive from him, because we keep his commandments and do those things that are pleasing in his sight. And this is his commandment: that we should believe on the name of his Son Jesus Christ and love one another, as he gave us commandment. Now he who keeps his commandments abides in him, and he in him. And by this we know that he abides in us, by the Spirit whom he has given us.

📖 1 John 4:7-19 (Love Is of God)*

Beloved, let us love one another, for love is of God; and everyone who loves is born of God and knows God. He who does not love does not know God, for God is love. In this the love of God was manifested toward us, that God has sent his only begotten Son into the world, that we might live through him. In this is love, not that we loved God, but that he loved us and sent his Son to be the propitiation for our sins. Beloved, if God so loved us, we also ought to love one another. No one has seen God at any time. If we love one

*From The New King James Version. Copyright © 1979, 1980, 1982, Thomas Nelson, Inc.

159

another, God abides in us, and his love has been perfected in us. By this we know that we abide in him, and he in us, because he has given us of his Spirit. And we have seen and testify that the Father has sent the Son as Savior of the world. Whoever confesses that Jesus is the Son of God, God abides in him, and he in God. And we have known and believed the love that God has for us. God is love, and he who abides in love abides in God, and God in him. Love has been perfected among us in this; that we may have boldness in the day of judgment; because as he is, so are we in this world. There is no fear in love; but perfect love casts out fear, because fear involves torment. But he who fears has not been made perfect in love. We love him because he first loved us.

📖 Revelation 19:1, 5-9 (Marriage Supper of the Lamb)*

After these things I heard a loud voice of a great multitude in heaven, saying, "Alleluia! Salvation and glory and honor and power to the Lord our God!"...Then a voice came from the throne, saying, "Praise our God, all you his servants and those who fear him, both small and great!" And I heard, as it were, the voice of a great multitude, as the sound of many waters and as the sound of mighty thunderings, saying, "Alleluia! For the Lord God Omnipotent reigns! Let us be glad and rejoice and give him glory, for the marriage of the Lamb has come, and his wife has made herself ready." And to her it was granted to be arrayed in fine linen, clean and bright, for the fine linen is the righteous acts of the saints. Then he said to me, "Write: 'blessed are those who are called to the marriage supper of the Lamb!'" And he said to me, "These are the true sayings of God."

*From The New King James Version. Copyright © 1979, 1980, 1982, Thomas Nelson, Inc.

📖 *Apocrypha*

📑 Tobit 7:9-17 (Marriage of Tobiah and Sarah)*

Raguel slaughtered a ram from the flock and gave them a cordial reception. When they had bathed and reclined to eat, Tobiah said to Raphael, "Brother Azariah, ask Raguel to let me marry my kinswoman Sarah." Raguel overheard the words; so he said to the boy: "Eat and drink and be merry tonight, for no man is more entitled to marry my daughter Sarah than you, brother. Besides, not even I have the right to give her to anyone but you, because you are my closest relative. But I will explain the situation to you very frankly. I have given her in marriage to seven men, all of whom were kinsmen of ours, and all died on the very night they approached her. But now, son, eat and drink. I am sure the Lord will look after you both." Tobiah answered, "I will eat and drink nothing until you set aside what belongs to me."

Raguel said to him: "I will do it. She is yours according to the decree of the Book of Moses. Your marriage to her has been decided in heaven! Take your kinswoman; from now on you are her love, and she is your beloved. She is yours today and ever after. And tonight, son, may the Lord of heaven prosper you both. May he grant you mercy and peace." Then Raguel called his daughter Sarah, and she came to him. He took her by the hand and gave her to Tobiah with the words: "Take her according to the law. According to the decree written in the Book of Moses she is your wife. Take her and bring her back safely to your father. And may the God of heaven grant both of you peace and prosperity." He then called her mother and told her to bring a scroll, so that he might draw up a marriage contract stating that he gave Sarah to Tobiah as his wife according to the decree of the Mosaic law. Her mother brought the scroll, and he drew up the contract, to which they affixed their seals.

---

*Selections from Tobit and Sirach are taken from the *New American Bible* Copyright © 1970 Confraternity of Christian Doctrine, Washington, DC. Used with permission. All rights reserved.

Afterward they began to eat and drink. Later Raguel called his wife Edna and said, "My love, prepare the other bedroom and bring the girl there. She went and made the bed in the room, as she was told, and brought the girl there. After she had cried over her, she wiped away the tears and said: "Be brave, my daughter. May the Lord of heaven grant you joy in place of your grief. Courage, my daughter." Then she left.

Tobit 8:5-7 (Prayer for Two Young Spouses)*

Sarah got up, and they started to pray and beg that deliverance might be theirs. He began with these words:

"Blessed are you, O God of our fathers;
Praised be your name forever and ever.
Let the heavens and all your creation praise you forever.
You made Adam and you gave him his wife Eve
To be his help and support;
and from these two the human race descended.
You said, 'It is not good for the man to be alone;
Let us make him a partner like himself.'
Now, Lord, you know that I take this wife of mine
not because of lust,
but for a noble purpose.
Call down your mercy on me and on her,
and allow us to live together to a happy old age."

Sirach 26:1-4, 13-18
(The Wife, Radiance of Her Home)*

Happy is the husband of a good wife,
twice-lengthened are his days;
A worthy wife brings joy to her husband,
peaceful and full is his life.
A good wife is a generous gift
bestowed upon him who fears the LORD;

Be he rich or poor, his heart is content,
and a smile is ever on his face...
A gracious wife delights her husband,
her thoughtfulness puts flesh on his bones;
A gift from the LORD is her governed speech,
and her firm virtue is of surpassing worth.
Choicest of blessings is a modest wife,
priceless her chaste person.
Like the sun rising in the LORD's heavens,
the beauty of a virtuous wife is the radiance of her home.
Like the light which shines above the holy lampstand,
are her beauty of face and graceful figure.
Golden columns on silver bases
are her shapely limbs and steady feet.

(*Selections from Tobit and Sirach are taken from the *New American Bible* Copyright © 1970 Confraternity of Christian Doctrine, Washington, DC. Used with permission. All rights reserved.)

📖 *Bahai Prayers*
(Bahai)

📖 *The Book of Mormon*
(The Church of Jesus Christ of Latter-day Saints)

📖 *Torah (Jewish)*

📖 *Qur'an (Muslim)*

📖 *Veda (Hindu)*

Secular

Secular readings may be chosen from essays, inspirational writings, novels, plays, poems, song lyrics, or other sources which express sentiment that has special meaning to you. There is an infinite variety of material from which to choose. Therefore, for secular readings to be a meaningful part of your ceremony, you will have to find an author or a verse that has special significance to you. Following are some examples of readings that may be applicable. Additional readings may be found in *Into the Garden: A Wedding Anthology* by Robert Hass and Stephen Mitchell, copyright © 1993 by HarperCollins Publishers, New York, NY.

Aristophanes — *The Peace: A Wedding Song*

author unknown — *God's Masterpiece*

Elizabeth Barrett Browning — *How Do I Love Thee? Sonnets From the Portuguese*

Robert Burns — *O, my luve's like a red, red rose*

e.e. cummings — *I carry your heart with me
if everything happens that can't be done
love is more thicker than forget*

Emily Dickinson — *Wild Nights — Wild Nights
Of all the Souls that stand create
It was a quiet way
I gave myself to Him
Alter! When the Hills Do*

John Donne — *The Anniversary
A Wedding Song on St. Valentine's Day*

John Fletcher — *Song*

Robert Frost — *The Master Speed*

Kahlil Gibran — *The Prophet, on Marriage*

D. H. Lawrence — *Fidelity*

Boris Pasternak — *A Wedding*

John Powell — *fully human, fully alive
why am i afraid to tell you who i am?
a reason to live! a reason to die*

Hugh and Gail Prather — *I Will Never Leave You*

Rainer Maria Rilke — *Love Song*

William Shakespeare — *Sonnet 116*

Walt Whitman — *We Two, How Long We Were Fool'd*

164

Apache song — "Now You Will Feel No Rain"

Hawaiian song — "Here All Seeking Is Over"

Navajo song — "The Night Chant"

Ojibway song — "Calling-One's-Own"

Wintu song — "Where Will You and I Sleep?"

❑ Cultural Traditions

Through ceremonies such as weddings, you celebrate events which you hold deep inside. Including cultural customs and traditions in your ceremony reflects your background and identity. Cultural traditions offer a variety of options for you to add elegance and beauty to your wedding ceremony, from traditional music, to wedding attire. They encourage you to acknowledge and appreciate your cultural heritage. They express who you are. They also allow you to simultaneously please yourselves and be respectful of your parents.

CHAPTER 14

When Are We Supposed to Do What?

Wedding planning is a tense experience for everyone involved. It represents significant judgments made by you and your future spouse. Making your wedding arrangements requires an extraordinary amount of planning, organizing, and attention to details. No matter how well-organized you normally are, planning your wedding is a major undertaking. You can be more deliberate in your plans, avoid more mistakes, and enjoy the task more if you allow sufficient time to prepare. (This is not to say that, if you are geared for speed, a beautiful wedding cannot be planned and performed in a short time without causing you a nervous breakdown or financial bankruptcy.) Careful preparation for a formal wedding normally takes nine to twelve months, particularly if you are going to be married in a highly populated area where the demand for popular sites, photographers, florists, caterers, and reception sites is greater. Even the simplest and most intimate wedding can require three months to arrange.

Furthermore, you will be performing all these activities with the added burden of this time being one of the most emotional periods of your lives. Therefore, you can use all the help you can get. The following timetable is designed to serve as a guideline and to prepare you for the responsibilities that lie ahead.

In order to keep all your wedding plans organized and readily accessible, you should start a file. You should make it a point to keep everything concerning your wedding plans in one place, arranged by categories.

In earlier times, the bride and her family traditionally planned the entire wedding. However, as with other wedding traditions, times have changed. The groom can work alongside you to help create a memorable wedding day. First, he can help decide on the style for the wedding and work on a realistic budget. Second, he can handle the traditional jobs and expenses for the groom, such as making the honeymoon arrangements and reserving the wedding night suite. Third, he can support you in the decisions you have made together and help resolve any disagreements which may arise between you and his family. Fourth, whatever he agrees to do, he should do cheerfully, helpfully, and with a smile. And fifth, he can work with you to decide how he may further help you.

By working together as a team in a spirit of cheerful cooperation, you and your partner will share the pride in a "job well done" when all your planning comes together on that magic day. But most importantly, you will have given yourselves a valuable head start on the teamwork vital to the success of your marriage in the years to come.

Since marriage ranks as one of life's most stressful changes, and since wedding planning is so hectic, it is important to your health to take some time to relax throughout the process. Take some time off from the planning chores. Spend a day with your fiancé doing something you both enjoy, and do *not* think about the wedding.

WEDDING PLANNING TIMETABLE

⧖ *Nine to Twelve Months Before the Wedding*

■ To Do Together

◆ *Ceremony*

❑ Select a target wedding date and time.

❑ After discussing your budget with both families, decide what kind of wedding to have: how formal, how big, how many guests, what kind of reception, what kind of music, and how expenses will be shared.

❑ Consult with your clergy/officiant concerning availability for your selected date and time.

❑ Begin engagement encounter retreat and/or marriage preparation counseling sessions before wedding plans become too firm to change and you become too pressured to continue.

❑ Schedule the photographer and videographer; make sure he/she is familiar with the ceremony site and any picture-taking restrictions.

◆ *Other*

❑ Choose and reserve wedding and reception sites and musicians/entertainers for your selected date and time. Decide on musical selections for the wedding.

❑ Choose the engagement ring together.

❑ Discuss how your money will be managed once you are married.

❑ Discuss ideas for your home, whether renting or buying, and begin household shopping.

❑ Plan your honeymoon: 1) Make plans and reservations as far in advance as possible; 2) Take time to investigate the location(s) you are considering; 3) Do not include too many locations; 4) Choose the location on the basis of shared interests, not personal preferences; and 5) Plan a honeymoon you can afford to enjoy, no matter where it is.

❑ Confer with/hire a wedding consultant, if desired (optional).

❑ Begin reading books about marriage and married life.

■ Bride

♦ *Ceremony*

❑ Decide on the color scheme for the wedding.

♦ *Other*

❑ Plan the reception menu.

❑ Check the catering facilities at the reception location; ask if the catering fee includes the wedding cake. If the reception is at someone's home, choose the caterer as soon as possible.

❑ Begin a wedding memory album.

■ Groom

♦ *Other*

❑ Decide which expenses you and your family will share with the bride and her family. Typically: flowers, beverages, and rehearsal dinner. Sharing reception and other costs is becoming increasingly common, but is not dictated by custom.

⧗ *Six Months Before*

■ To Do Together

♦ *Ceremony*

❑ Visit your clergy/officiant performing the ceremony.

❑ Book your musicians for both the ceremony and reception.

- ### *Other*

  - ❑ Select china, crystal, silver, linens and other items and register your selections with the bridal gift registries at your favorite stores.

  - ❑ Announce your engagement in the newspaper.

  - ❑ Select your wedding rings and engraved inscriptions for each.

■ Bride

- ### *Ceremony*

  - ❑ Choose and order your wedding dress, veil, and accessories, if the wedding is formal. Remember that you may need a fitting and adjustment.

  - ❑ Choose your honor attendant, bridesmaids, junior bridesmaids (if any), and flower girl. Choose and order dresses and accessories for them that are versatile enough for post-wedding parties.

  - ❑ Select the florist and discuss the color scheme and flower selection.

  - ❑ Tell both mothers the wedding color scheme.

  - ❑ Let the groom's mother know how many guests she may invite, and by what date you need her guest list.

■ Groom

- ### *Ceremony*

  - ❑ Confirm with the bride's mother how many guests you may invite, then work out your guest list with your own family.

  - ❑ Begin shopping for men's wedding attire.

- ### *Other*

  - ❑ Start making honeymoon arrangements. Check your passports, visas, and inoculations if you will be leaving the country.

❑ Reserve the wedding night suite.

⧖ *Three Months Before*

■ To Do Together

◆ *Ceremony*

❑ Plan wedding and reception music. Tape any pre-recorded music that may be used (optional).

❑ Reserve the wedding and reception rental items.

❑ Write and review your wedding ceremony/vows (optional).

❑ Arrange for parking attendants at the wedding ceremony and/or reception (optional).

◆ *Other*

❑ Arrange for physical examinations, blood tests, and needed inoculations. Visit dentists, dermatologists, and eye doctors as appropriate, if it is anywhere near your regular check-up time.

❑ Arrange legal matters, such as wills, name changes on legal documents, prenuptial agreements, and legal guardianship of children from any previous marriage (if any).

❑ Purchase accessories such as toasting goblets, cake knife, ring pillow, garter, guest book, flower girl's basket, etc.

❑ Make sure the birth control method you will be or are currently using is satisfactory to both of you.

❑ Decide on decor and furnishings for your new house or apartment.

❑ Begin reading books about sexual relations in marriage.

■ **Bride**

◆ *Ceremony*

❏ Complete your guest list and announcement-only list. Check the groom's list for duplications.

❏ Order your invitations and announcements. Buy the envelopes early so they can be addressed and ready to mail when the printed invitations arrive. Design a map showing the wedding/reception locations for insertion with the invitations.

❏ Reserve a limousine for wedding party.

❏ Finalize plans for the wedding rehearsal.

❏ Make your hair and beauty preparation appointment (usually for wedding day morning). Have the hairdresser, cosmetologist, or aesthetician come to where you will be dressing, if possible.

❏ Discuss all details of the ceremony (flowers, music, photography, special carpeting, etc.) with the responsible suppliers.

❏ If you are wearing an heirloom gown, select a dry cleaner who is experienced in cleaning vintage clothes and drop it off to be cleaned and pressed.

◆ *Other*

❏ If you want personal stationery, order it now.

❏ Plan and buy your trousseau: clothes, cosmetics and the like.

❏ Plan your bridal portrait date for as soon as possible after delivery of your wedding dress.

❏ Discuss all details of your reception with the person who will be in charge and present. Make sure the person you talk to will be present at the reception.

❏ Reserve any rental equipment.

❏ If the wedding cake is not included by the caterer,

select a baker and order the cake.

❑ Arrange for time off from work for the wedding and honeymoon.

■ Groom

◆ *Ceremony*

❑ Finish your guest list and give it to the bride.

❑ Select your best man and line up your groomsmen, ushers, junior groomsmen (if any), ring bearer, and pages (if any). Suggest the place where they can order their wedding attire.

◆ *Other*

❑ Check and replenish your wardrobe.

❑ Complete your honeymoon reservations and pick up tickets.

❑ Arrange time off from work for the wedding and honeymoon.

⧗ *One Month Before*

■ To Do Together

◆ *Ceremony*

❑ Obtain your marriage license.

❑ Pick up your wedding ring(s).

❑ Have the florist visit the ceremony/reception sites to plan the flower arrangements.

❑ Ask a close friend or relative to attend to the wedding guest book.

◆ *Other*

❑ If exchanging wedding gifts, buy them now.

❑ Purchase gifts for organist/musicians (optional).

❑ Secure and pre-pay for accommodations for wedding members from out of town.

❑ Prepare an information kit for out-of-town guests.

❑ Arrange transportation for out-of-town wedding party members and guests.

■ Bride

◆ *Ceremony*

❑ Take a complete invitation with the response envelope and all enclosures to the post office to be weighed for proper postage.

❑ Mail invitations so they arrive three weeks before the wedding.

❑ Select and order flowers.

❑ Have the final fitting of your wedding dress, veil, and accessories, and confirm your wedding portrait date.

❑ Select your wedding ring (if you have not already done so) with the groom. If a double-ring ceremony is planned, arrange to pick up and pay for the groom's ring.

◆ *Other*

❑ Have your formal bridal portrait taken.

❑ Purchase wedding gift for groom (optional).

❑ Buy gifts for your flower girl, junior bridesmaids, bridesmaids, and a special gift for your honor attendant.

❑ Arrange the bridesmaids' luncheon or dinner.

❑ Keep writing thank you notes for later mailing.

❑ Arrange your change of name and address (if you are changing them) on business records and personal documents.

■ **Groom**

◆ *Ceremony*

❑ Do a final check of the status of all wedding attire for you, your best man, groomsmen, ushers, junior groomsmen (if any), ring bearer, and pages, if any.

❑ Order boutonnieres and flowers for the wedding party and for the two mothers.

◆ *Other*

❑ Arrange the rehearsal dinner if you or your family are giving it.

❑ Check your health and life insurance. Make changes to reflect your married status, if desired.

❑ Make sure all legal, medical, and religious documents are in order.

❑ Purchase wedding gift for bride (optional).

❑ Buy gifts for the ring bearer, groomsmen, ushers, junior groomsmen, pages, and a special gift for your best man.

⧗ *Two Weeks Before*

■ **To Do Together**

◆ *Ceremony*

❑ Meet with the photographer/videographer and provide a list of special pictures or events you want taken.

❑ Remind each member of the wedding party of the date, time, and location of the rehearsal.

❑ Contact any guests who have not responded to their invitations.

◆ *Other*

❏ Obtain wedding questionnaire forms from your local newspaper(s). For newspapers not using forms, write your announcement, keeping it brief and factual.

■ **Bride**

◆ *Ceremony*

❏ With your hairdresser or cosmetologist, plan both your wedding hairdo and a workable routine for honeymoon hair/beauty care. Bring along your headpiece or veil to help select the right hair style. If you plan to have your hair done on or near the wedding day, reconfirm the appointment.

◆ *Other*

❏ Complete trousseau shopping. Transfer a small amount of cosmetics to plastic containers for your honeymoon trip.

❏ Continue writing thank-you notes.

■ **Grooms**

◆ *Ceremony*

❏ Make the arrangements for your best man to transport you and your bride from the reception to the airport, ship terminal, train station, or other honeymoon departure point on time. If you are driving, plan now to have him carry an extra set of your car keys on the wedding day.

⧗ *One Week Before*

■ **To Do Together**

◆ *Ceremony*

❏ Assign the tasks to be performed on the wedding day to your wedding party.

❏ Attend the rehearsal and rehearsal dinner.

■ **Bride**

◆ *Ceremony*

❏ Review rehearsal procedures with the groom and the clergy / officiant.

❏ Remind your honor attendant, bridesmaids, junior bridesmaids, and flower girl of the rehearsal and dinner.

❏ Provide the wedding party and out-of-town guests with final arrangements for the rehearsal, rehearsal dinner, ceremony, and reception.

❏ Check on the arrival of gowns and trousseau items; check and double check delivery instructions for wedding, reception and honeymoon items.

❏ Practice applying your make-up and determine the amount of time you will require to apply it on the wedding day.

❏ Conduct a final check of the ceremony and reception details with everyone concerned.

◆ *Other*

❏ Appoint a charge d'affaires (not a member of your immediate family) to attend to the last-minute details, receive wires, expedite serving at the reception, etc.

❏ Hold the bridesmaids' luncheon or dinner.

❏ Begin packing for your honeymoon; have your going-away clothes pressed and ready.

❏ Be sure announcements (if any) are ready for your parents to mail right after the wedding.

❏ Deliver completed wedding forms / written announcements to the newspaper(s).

❑ Give the caterer (if you are using one) a final guest count estimate for the reception and plan the seating arrangements.

❑ Arrange the transportation of your gifts and possessions to your new home.

❑ Continue writing thank-you notes (time permitting).

❑ Enjoy your bachelorette party.

❑ Make the day before the wedding your relaxation day: treat yourself to a facial, massage, manicure, and pedicure.

❑ Present gifts to attendants at either the bridesmaids' luncheon or the rehearsal dinner.

❑ Prepare Bride's Emergency Kit (See table 14-1).

Table 14-1, Bride's Emergency Kit

A little advance planning and preparation can help prevent last-minute mishaps from becoming major crises. Sonja Kueppers compiled the following list of items to include in a Bride's Emergency Kit based upon discussions among brides-to-be on the Internet (on alt.wedding and soc.couples.wedding). The kit container can be anything from a shopping bag to an overnight bag. Once everything is pulled together, the kit is left in the bride's dressing room or other place for easy access at the wedding site. It should also be taken to the reception by a member of the wedding party.

Health Items

- antacids
- antihistamines

- Band-Aids & antiseptic
- hard candy & Life Savers
- headache remedies
- prescription medications
- smelling salts
- sunscreen

- tampons & pads

Attire

- buttons
- clear nail polish (for runs in hose)
- earring backs
- flat shoes or ballet slippers
- iron
- pantyhose (extras)
- safety pins
- sewing kit (with thread for all dresses)
- tape (hem mending)
- "throw-away" garter

Beauty/Grooming

- dusting powder
- facial tissue
- hair spray, brush, barrettes and/or bobby pins
- hand lotion and handi-wipes
- hand towel (small)

- make-up
- nail polish remover
- toothbrush and toothpaste

Miscellaneous

- bottled drinking water
- coins for pay telephone
- directions to ceremony/reception
- flashlight (small)
- telephone numbers (service people)

- **Groom**

  - *Ceremony*

    - ❑ Remind your best man, groomsmen/ushers, junior groomsmen, ring bearer, and pages of the rehearsal and dinner.
    - ❑ Put the fee for the clergy/officiant in a sealed envelope and give it to your best man.
    - ❑ Make sure you have the marriage license and rings and give them to your best man *before* the ceremony.
    - ❑ Have your hair trimmed and get a manicure.

  - *Other*

    - ❑ Confirm reservations and start packing for your honeymoon.
    - ❑ Move your possessions to your new home, if necessary.
    - ❑ Enjoy your bachelor party.
    - ❑ Present gifts to the groomsmen/ushers at either the bachelor party or rehearsal dinner.

⌛ *Wedding Day*

- **Bride**

  - *Ceremony*

    - ❑ Check with the florist to ensure that the flowers will be delivered on time.
    - ❑ Apply your make-up, style your hair, and start dressing at least 2½ hours before the ceremony.
    - ❑ Arrive at the ceremony site (church, courthouse, or wherever ceremony is held) on time.

- **Groom**

  - *Ceremony*

    - ❑ Make sure the best man has the rings, the marriage license, the clergy/officiant fee, and an extra set of your car keys.

❑ Start dressing at least 1½ hours before the ceremony.

❑ Arrive at the ceremony site (church, courthouse, or wherever ceremony is held) on time.

⧖ *After the Wedding*

◆ *Other*

❑ Write and mail all thank-you notes as soon as possible.

❑ Take care of name changes and legal affairs as soon as possible.

Table 14-2, Sample Ceremony Countdown

⏱ **Two to Three Hours Before** — The bride, her mother, and attendants begin dressing.

⏱ **One Hour Before** — Any bridesmaids who have dressed elsewhere gather at the bride's house to pick up their flowers, pose for pictures, and assemble for transportation to the ceremony site.

The honor attendant checks the attire of the bridesmaids.

The best man makes sure the ushers understand their instructions and checks their attire.

The florist arrives at the site and sets up the flower arrangements.

⏱ **Forty-Five Minutes Before** — The ushers arrive at the site, pin on their boutonnieres, review their duties and the seating instructions, and gather near the vestibule or entrance to greet arriving guests.

⏱ **Thirty Minutes Before** — The organist begins playing prelude music while the ushers escort guests to their seats.

The groom and best man arrive at the site and wait in the vestry or designated room out of sight. The clergy/officiant makes certain that the best man has brought the marriage license, receives the fee from the best man, and issues any last-minute instructions.

The photographer/videographer arrives at the site, sets up, and starts taking pictures.

⏱ **Fifteen Minutes Before** — The bride, her parents, and attendants arrive at the site and wait in the vestibule or rear of the site while relatives and guests are seated. If possible, the bride, her father/escort, and attendants go to a room adjacent to the vestibule and stay out of sight. The clergy/officiant goes over any last-minute details.

○ **Five to Ten Minutes Before** — The groom's relatives and mother arrive at the site and are seated.

○ **Two to Five Minutes Before** — The bride's relatives and mother are seated. The bride's mother is the last person to be seated.

The bride, her father/escort, and attendants assemble in the vestibule or rear of the site.

○ **One to Two Minutes Before** — Two ushers attach the aisle ribbons and lay the aisle carpet, then return to the rear of the site (vestibule) to take their places in the processional.

○ **Ceremony Time** — The clergy/officiant, the groom, and the best man take their places, the processional begins, and all rise to watch the bride enter.

Table 14-3, Wedding Ceremony Timetable Checklist

⏳ 9-12 Months Before Wedding

❑ Select tentative wedding date and time.

❑ Choose and reserve wedding location.

❑ Select photographer/videographer.

❑ Hire wedding consultant (optional).

❑ Decide on color scheme.

⏳ 6 Months Before Wedding

❑ Visit clergy/officiant about the suitability of the date you have tentatively selected and marriage counseling.

❑ Select wedding rings.

❑ Book musicians for ceremony.

❑ Order wedding dress and accessories.

❑ Choose bride's attendants.

❑ Order attendants' dresses and accessories.

❑ Select florist.

⏳ 3 Months Before Wedding

❑ Plan wedding music.

❑ Write wedding ceremony/vows.

❑ Arrange parking attendants for ceremony.

❑ Reserve limousine for bridal party.

❑ Finalize wedding rehearsal plans.

❑ Discuss ceremony details with suppliers.

❑ Make hair/beauty preparation appointments.

❑ Order wedding cake.

- ❏ Select groomsmen.
- ❏ Select groomsmen's attire.
- ❏ Order wedding invitations and announcements.

⏳ 1 Month Before Wedding

- ❏ Obtain marriage license.
- ❏ Pick up weddings rings.
- ❏ Mail wedding invitations.
- ❏ Select/order flowers.
- ❏ Have final wedding dress fitting.
- ❏ Arrange rehearsal dinner.
- ❏ Check status of bride's attendants and groomsmen's attire.

⏳ 2 Weeks Before Wedding

- ❏ Remind wedding party of date, time, and location of rehearsal.

⏳ 1 Week Before Wedding

- ❏ Assign wedding party ceremony tasks.
- ❏ Attend rehearsal/rehearsal dinner.
- ❏ Appoint someone to handle last-minute details.
- ❏ Conduct final check of ceremony details.
- ❏ Give best man the clergy/officiant fee, marriage license, and rings for safekeeping.

⏳ Wedding Day

- ❏ Check florist to ensure flowers are delivered on time.
- ❏ Make sure best man has clergy/officiant fee, marriage license, and rings.
- ❏ Arrive at ceremony site on time.

ᴄ𝒲ho ᴄᗪoes ᴄ𝒲hat?

ᴄ𝒥raditionally, certain responsibilities have been established for each member of the wedding party and the guests. This chapter discusses those responsibilities to serve as a guide for delegating the various duties associated with planning and conducting a wedding. Please bear in mind that your individual circumstances, such as the size of the wedding, your age, and your financial situation, may cause shifts in those responsibilities.

❐ Wedding Expenses

Money does matter. Unless you are independently wealthy, financial realities will require making choices. The choices that you make set the tone and reflect your particular wedding style.

Under traditional arrangements, the bride's family paid most of the wedding expenses. But the escalating costs associated with conducting a wedding are causing couples and their families to devise more practical financial arrangements. The trend today is for the financial obligations associated with a wedding to be shared — not only by the respective families, but also by the bride and groom themselves.

At the time the wedding is being planned, the two of you, as well as both your families, should meet to discuss the financial obligations and/or limitations of the wedding. This will prevent misunderstandings later.

Many couples and their families are finding new ways of sharing expenses rather than sacrificing their ideas of the "perfect" wedding celebration and reception. Ways of sharing expenses include: both families sharing the costs equally; the bride's family paying the larger share but the groom's family making a major contribution; the groom's family paying the larger share but the bride's family making a major contribution; the wedding couple assuming a third of the cost; and the wedding couple absorbing all or most of the costs themselves. So as you can see, today there really are no absolute standard rules governing how you and your families arrange wedding expenses.

If it is the bride's first marriage, or if she was widowed or divorced at an early age, her parents may offer to pay for the wedding.

If the groom and/or his parents are financially willing and able, they may offer at any time to pay part, half, or all of the wedding expenses. This is true of the couple as well.

If both the bride and groom have been previously married, they normally split the wedding expenses between themselves.

Remember that the reception usually accounts for up to fifty percent of the total cost of the wedding. If it is necessary to reduce costs, the reception may be the place to start, beginning with the location and/or the number of guests.

The following table (on page 191) shows you the approximate percentage that each major item represents of the total wedding expenses. These percentages are offered for planning purposes only. Remember that your wedding expenses will vary based upon the decisions you make.

Table 15-1, Sample Allocation of Wedding Expenses

Attire	**19.0%**
Bride	9.0%
Bride's attendants	7.5%
Groom & attendants	2.5%
Ceremony	**4.5%**
Clergy/Officiant	1.5%
Site	2.0%
Music	1.0%
Flowers	**5.0%**
Miscellaneous	**4.5%**
Photographer/Videographer	**9.0%**
Reception	**44.5%**
Rings	**13.5%**
	100.0%

❐ Bride's Responsibilities

❑ Select tentative wedding date with groom.

❑ Choose and reserve wedding location with groom.

❑ Select musicians/wedding music with groom.

❑ Select bridal attendants.

❑ Select florist/flowers.

❑ Order wedding cake.

❑ Decide wedding color scheme.

❑ Select wedding ensemble.

❑ Select attendants' attire.

❑ Arrange ceremony parking attendants with groom (optional).

❑ Purchase groom's wedding ring for a double-ring ceremony.

❑ Purchase gifts for maid of honor, attendants, and flower girl.

❑ Purchase groom's wedding gift (optional).

❑ Arrange personal medical examination and blood test.

❑ Order personal stationery (optional).

❑ Obtain and pack personal luggage.

❑ Sign gift registry for wedding present selections.

❑ Host bridesmaids' luncheon or party (optional, if not hosted by bride's family).

❑ Arrange lodging for out-of-town bridesmaids (optional, if not arranged by bride's family).

❑ Write wedding vows and select readings with groom (optional).

❑ Arrive promptly for the rehearsal and the wedding.

❑ Take part in wedding processional/recessional.

❑ Pose for photographs after the ceremony.

❑ Stand in receiving line.

❑ Bride's Family's Responsibilities

❑ Provide bride's personal and household trousseau.

❑ Provide bride's wedding ensemble (dress, headpiece, and accessories).

❑ Order wedding invitations and enclosure cards.

❑ Order wedding announcements.

❑ Provide wedding guest book.

❑ Arrange engagement and wedding photographs.

❑ Purchase bouquets for honor attendant, bridesmaids, junior bridesmaids, and flower girls (optional, when not paid for by the groom or groom's family).

❑ Purchase gifts for musicians / organist.

❑ Provide wedding site expenses (except the clergy / officiant's fee); sanctuary or facility rental fees; organist, soloist, choir or musicians' fees; decorations, aisle carpet, and flowers; and the custodian.

❑ Host bridal or rehearsal dinner (if not hosted by the groom's family).

❑ Host bridesmaids' luncheon (optional).

❑ Arrange lodging for out-of-town bridal attendants and special guests.

❑ Arrive promptly at rehearsal and wedding ceremony.

❑ Provide transportation of bridal party from bride's house to ceremony and reception sites.

❑ Pose with wedding party for photographs after ceremony.

❑ Host wedding reception (including music, beverages, catering, flowers / decorations, gratuities and professional services).

❑ Mingle with guests at reception.

❑ Give a wedding gift to the bride and groom from the family.

❑ Obtain own wedding attire.

❑ Pay bridal consultant's fee (optional).

❑ Bride's Mother's Responsibilities

❑ Assist bride in compiling guest list and arranging details of the ceremony and reception.

❑ Keep track of wedding gifts.

❑ Display gifts in an attractive and safe place.

❑ Keep the bride's father and groom's parents up to date on the progress of the planning.

❑ Is invited to all showers.

❑ Has first choice on wedding attire and informs groom's mother of her selection so that their dresses will be the same length and of complementary color.

❑ Is last person seated before the ceremony and first person escorted out after the recessional.

❑ Cue guests to stand for the processional.

❑ Sit in place of honor at the parents' table during reception.

❑ Act as hostess of the wedding and reception and is first on the receiving line to greet guests.

❒ Bride's Father's Responsibilities

❑ Select attire that blends with that of the groom, best man, groomsmen and ushers.

❑ Ride to ceremony site with bride.

❑ Escort bride down the aisle and give her away or bless the marriage.

❑ Act as host of the reception.

❑ Stand in receiving line when very formal wedding and/or when groom's parents are not acquainted with most guests (optional).

❑ Dance with bride at reception.

❒ Groom's Responsibilities

❑ Select tentative wedding date and time with bride.

❑ Choose and reserve wedding location with bride.

❑ Select musicians/wedding music with bride.

❑ Select attendants.

❑ Arrange ceremony parking attendants with bride (optional).

❑ Select bride's engagement and wedding rings.

❑ Select and obtain own wedding attire.

❑ Select attendants' attire.

❑ Obtain marriage license.

❑ Purchase bride's bouquet and going-away corsage,

bridesmaids' bouquets, boutonnieres for the men, and corsages for both mothers and grandmothers.

❑ Arrange medical examination and blood test.

❑ Purchase a gift for bride.

❑ Purchase gifts for best man, groomsmen, ushers, and ring bearer; groom may also provide accessories (ties and gloves) for male attendants and both fathers in a strictly formal wedding (optional).

❑ Obtain luggage and necessities for personal wardrobe.

❑ Arrange accommodations for out-of-town groomsmen and special guests (optional, if not arranged by groom's family).

❑ Host groomsmen's party or dinner (optional).

❑ Pay clergy/officiant's fee (for a judge, a suitable gift may be sufficient).

❑ Write wedding vows and select readings with bride (optional).

❑ Arrive promptly for rehearsal and wedding.

❑ Escort bride during recessional.

❑ Stand in receiving line.

❑ Pose for photographs after the ceremony.

❑ Set up all the honeymoon arrangements and pay expenses.

❐ Groom's Family's Responsibilities

❑ Conform to the wedding plans set by bride's parents.

❑ Obtain their own wedding attire.

❑ Pay personal travel expenses and hotel bills.

❑ Arrange lodging for groom's out-of-town attendants and special guests.

❑ Host bridal (or rehearsal) dinner.

❑ Purchase bouquets for honor attendant, bridesmaids,

junior bridesmaids, and flower girl (optional, when not paid for by groom).

❏ Give a wedding gift to the bride and groom from the family.

❏ Arrive promptly at the wedding.

❏ Pose for photographs with wedding party after ceremony.

❏ Mingle with guests at reception.

❏ Provide beverages at reception (optional).

❏ Groom's Mother's Responsibilities

❏ Compile guest list for the groom's side.

❏ Is invited to all showers.

❏ Consult with bride's mother on proper wedding attire and select attire that complements bride's mother's attire.

❏ Is invited to the rehearsal dinner (if not hosted by the groom's parents).

❏ Stand next to bride's mother in reception line (when bride's father is not in the line).

❏ Dance with groom at reception.

❏ Groom's Father's Responsibilities

❏ Consult with bride's father on proper wedding attire.

❏ Is invited to the rehearsal dinner (if not hosted by the groom's parents).

❏ Stand next to bride in the receiving line when very formal wedding and/or when groom's parents are not acquainted with most guests (optional).

❏ Maid/Matron of Honor's Responsibilities

❏ Assist bride whenever she can.

❏ Help bride address invitations, announcements, and thank-you envelopes.

❑ Obtain wedding attire (conforms to bride's selection).

❑ Attend all pre-wedding parties.

❑ Help bride dress.

❑ Ensure that bridesmaids are ready on time and properly attired.

❑ Arrive promptly for rehearsal and wedding.

❑ Ride to ceremony with the bride (optional).

❑ Instruct and keep track of flower girl during ceremony.

❑ Precede bride and her father/escort down the aisle during the processional.

❑ Carry a handkerchief during wedding service and discreetly give to bride if needed.

❑ Adjust veil and train of bride's wedding dress.

❑ Accompany bride at altar.

❑ Hold bride's bouquet during ceremony.

❑ Hold and pass groom's ring to the bride (in a double ring ceremony).

❑ Escorted by best man during recessional.

❑ Sign marriage certificate and license.

❑ Pose for photographs with wedding party after ceremony.

❑ Stand next to groom in the receiving line.

❑ Sit to the left of the groom at the bride's table during reception.

❑ Dance with the groom at the reception (after the mothers).

❑ Help bride change after the reception.

❑ Give a wedding gift to the bride and groom.

❑ Help record wedding gifts.

❑ Bridesmaids' Responsibilities

❑ Obtain own wedding attire (conforms to bride's selection).

❑ Attend all pre-wedding parties.

❑ Stand ready to help the bride in any way possible.

❑ Entertain the bride with showers, luncheons or teas.

❑ Arrange own transportation to wedding site unless bride's family has made arrangements to transport the bride and her attendants to the site.

❑ Arrive promptly for rehearsal and wedding.

❑ Be ready at least a half hour before appointed time for photographs in order to prevent the party from waiting.

❑ Take part in the processional and stand at the bride's side during ceremony.

❑ Escorted by groomsmen during recessional.

❑ Pose for photographs with the wedding party after ceremony.

❑ Stand in receiving line after ceremony.

❑ Sit next to groomsmen/ushers at the bride's table during reception.

❑ Give bride and groom a wedding gift (individually, not as a group).

❒ Junior Bridesmaids' Responsibilities (Optional)

❑ Obtain own wedding attire (which must be similar in style to that of the bridesmaids but appropriate to their age).

❑ Arrive promptly at rehearsal and ceremony.

❑ Be ready at least a half hour before appointed time for photographs in order to prevent the wedding party from waiting.

❑ Arrange own transportation to wedding site (usually with parents).

❑ Take part in the processional behind the bridesmaids and in front of the honor attendant.

❑ Escorted by junior ushers, if any, during recessional.

❑ Pose for photographs with wedding party after ceremony.

❑ Stand in receiving line after ceremony.

❑ Best Man's Responsibilities

❑ Serve as groom's personal aide and advisor.

❑ Host bachelor party or dinner.

❑ Obtain own wedding attire (conforms to groom's selection).

❑ Act as chief of staff at wedding.

❑ Appoint head usher; brief ushers on special seating arrangements; and see that ushers are properly attired.

❑ Take charge of bride's wedding ring.

❑ Keep track of the marriage license.

❑ Secure clergy/officiant's fee from groom, seal in an envelope, and hand to clergy/officiant after ceremony.

❑ Help groom dress; see that groom is properly attired; and ensure that groom arrives at ceremony site on time.

❑ Instruct and keep track of ring bearer during ceremony.

❑ Arrive promptly at rehearsal and ceremony.

❑ Accompany groom to ceremony and wait for beginning of ceremony with groom.

❑ Enter with clergy/officiant and groom prior to processional.

❑ Carry a handkerchief during wedding service and discreetly give to groom if needed.

❑ Accompany groom at altar.

❑ Pass bride's ring to groom.

❑ Escort honor attendant during recessional.

- ❑ Sign marriage certificate and license.
- ❑ Pose for photographs with wedding party after ceremony.
- ❑ Sit to the right of bride at the bride's table during reception.
- ❑ Dance with bride, her mother, each bridesmaid, and his mother (if present).
- ❑ Is the first person to toast the bride and groom.
- ❑ Assemble groom's parents after reception so that they can say good-bye and assure safe honeymoon departure for the couple.
- ❑ Help groom change clothes after reception.
- ❑ Give a wedding gift to the bride and groom.
- ❑ Ensure that all rented men's attire is returned on time.

❏ Groomsmen's Responsibilities

- ❑ Obtain own wedding attire (conforms to groom's selection).
- ❑ Help the best man hold bachelor party for the groom.
- ❑ Obtain a wedding gift for the bride and groom.
- ❑ Arrive promptly for rehearsal.
- ❑ Arrive at least forty-five minutes to an hour before ceremony.
- ❑ Lead the processional (optional).
- ❑ Escort bridesmaids during recessional.
- ❑ Pose for photographs with wedding party after ceremony.
- ❑ Do *not* stand in reception line.
- ❑ Sit next to the bridesmaids at the bride's table during reception.
- ❑ Act as escorts to bridesmaids after ceremony and provide transportation for bridesmaids to the reception (if other arrangements have not been made).

❑ Assist bride's parents in hosting the reception party as required.

❑ Junior Groomsmen's Responsibilities (Optional)

❑ Obtain own wedding attire (which must be similar in style to that of the ushers).

❑ Arrive promptly at rehearsal and ceremony.

❑ Must be ready at least a half hour before appointed time to prevent the wedding party from waiting.

❑ Arrange own transportation to wedding site (usually with parents).

❑ Light candles, lay aisle carpet, and/or attach aisle ribbons prior to the processional, and extinguish candles and remove the aisle ribbons and/or aisle carpet after the recessional.

❑ Take part in the processional behind the ushers and in front of the bridesmaids.

❑ Escort junior bridesmaids, if any.

❑ Pose for photographs with wedding party after ceremony.

❑ Flower Girl's Responsibilities (Optional)

❑ Obtain own wedding attire (which must complement the bridesmaids' attire but be appropriate to her age).

❑ Arrive promptly for rehearsal and ceremony.

❑ Arrange own transportation to wedding site (usually with parents).

❑ Carry flowers (bouquet, nosegay, or basket of rose petals).

❑ Walk immediately before the bride in the processional.

❑ Walk with the ring bearer in the recessional.

❑ Pose for photographs with wedding party after ceremony.

❒ Ring Bearer's Responsibilities (Optional)

❑ Obtain own wedding attire (which is similar to that of the groomsmen).

❑ Arrive promptly for rehearsal and ceremony.

❑ Arrange own transportation to wedding site (usually with parents).

❑ Carry ceremonial rings (which are usually sewn to a silk cushion).

❑ Walk immediately before the flower girl in the processional.

❑ Walk with the flower girl in the recessional.

❑ Pose for photographs with wedding party after ceremony.

❒ Pages' or Train Bearers' Responsibilities — Normally Pairs (Optional)

❑ Obtain own wedding attire (which is similar to that of the ushers).

❑ Arrange own transportation to wedding site (usually with parents).

❑ Arrive promptly for rehearsal and wedding ceremony.

❑ Carry bride's wedding dress train during processional and recessional (only needed if the bride's dress train is long, e.g. cathedral or extended cathedral length).

❑ Are usually young boys but can be girls.

❑ Pose for photographs with the wedding party after the ceremony.

❒ Guests

❑ Respond to the formal wedding invitation.

❑ Pay any travel expenses and hotel bills they incur.

❑ Consult with bride's mother about the couple's gift needs.

❏ Give a wedding gift to the bride and groom (this applies to those guests invited to both the wedding ceremony and reception — guests invited only to the ceremony are not obligated to provide a gift).

❏ Dress appropriately for the style of the wedding.

❏ Be on time for the ceremony (about a half hour before the ceremony, or fifteen minutes for guests with reserved seats). It is not fashionable to be late.

❏ Allow additional travel time to compensate for inclement weather, traffic, and unfamiliar locations.

❏ Seat themselves in the rear of the sanctuary or site if they arrive after the ceremony has begun.

❏ Follow lead of bride's family in standing for the processional and during the service, but should not attempt to perform church rituals they are unfamiliar with.

❏ Remain seated after the recessional until the ushers have escorted the families of the bride and groom out of the wedding site.

❏ Pass along the receiving line, shaking hands with everyone and making pleasant comments about the ceremony.

❏ Wish the bride and groom well.

❏ Remain at reception as long as the bride and groom, or at least until the cake cutting.

■ = Primary
O = Optional

TABLE 15-2, WEDDING CEREMONY RESPONSIBILITIES

Task	Bride	Bride's Family	Bride's Mother	Bride's Father	Groom	Groom's Family	Groom's Mother	Groom's Father	Maid/Matron of Honor	Bridesmaids	Junior Bridesmaids	Best Man	Groomsmen	Junior Groomsmen	Flower Girl	Ring Bearer	Page/Train Bearer	Guest
Select tentative wedding date	■				■													
Choose and reserve wedding site	■				■													
Select musicians/wedding music	■				■													
Select bride's attendants	■																	
Select florists/flowers	■																	
Decide wedding color scheme	■				■													
Select bride's wedding ensemble	■																	
Select attendants' attire	■				■													
Arrange ceremony parking attendants	O				O													
Purchase groom's ring	■																	
Purchase gifts for bride's attendants	■																	
Purchase gift for groom	O																	
Arrange medical examination and blood test	O				■													
Write wedding vows/ceremony	O				O													
Arrive at rehearsal/wedding on time	■	■			■	■			■	■	■	■	■	■	■	■	■	
Take part in wedding processional/recessional	■			■ (P)	■ (R)	■			■	■	■	■	■	■	■	■	■	
Pose for photographs after the ceremony	■				■	■	■		■	■	O	■	■	■	■	■	■	
Stand in receiving line			■				■	O	■									
Provide bride's wedding ensemble		■																
Order wedding invitations and enclosure cards		■																
Order wedding announcements		■																
Provide wedding guest book		■																
Arrange engagement and wedding photographs		■																
Purchase gifts for musicians/organist		■																
Provide wedding site expenses		■																
Host bridal or rehearsal dinner		O				■												
Arrange out-of-town bridal attendants and special guest accommodations	O	■																
Provide bridal party transportation to ceremony/reception		■																
Give wedding gift to bride and groom		■				■			■	■		■	■			■	■	■
Obtain personal wedding attire		■				■			■	■	■	■	■	■	■	■	■	■
Pay bridal consultant	O																	
Assist bride with guest list and arrangements			■															

TABLE 15-2, WEDDING CEREMONY RESPONSIBILITIES (continued)

■ = Primary O = Optional

Task	Bride	Bride's Family	Bride's Mother	Bride's Father	Groom	Groom's Family	Groom's Mother	Groom's Father	Maid/Matron of Honor	Brides-maids	Junior Brides-maids	Best Man	Grooms-men	Junior Grooms-men	Flower Girl	Ring Bearer	Page/Train Bearer	Guest
Keep track of and safeguard wedding gifts			■															
Keep bride's father and groom's parents informed			■															
Has first choice on personal wedding attire			■															
Is last person seated at ceremony			■															
Cue guests to stand for processional																		
Act as wedding hostess			■															
Select attire to blend with groom and groomsmen				■														
Ride to ceremony with bride				■					O									
Escort bride during processional				■														
Select groom's attendants					■													
Select bride's engagement and wedding rings					■													
Obtain marriage license					■													
Purchase wedding party bouquets and boutonniere		O			O													
Purchase gift for bride					■													
Purchase gifts for groom's attendants					■	■												
Arrange out-of-town groomsmen and special guests accommodations					O													
Pay clergy/officiant fee					■													
Conform to wedding plans						■												
Pay personal travel expenses						■											■	
Compile groom's guest list							■											
Consult bride's mother/father on attire							■	■										
Assist bride										■								
Help address invitations, announcements, and thank-you's									■									
Help bride dress									■									
Ensure bridesmaids are on time and properly attired									■									
Instruct and keep track of flower girl(s)									■									
Precede bride in processional									■									
Carry handkerchief during ceremony for bride/groom									■									
Adjust bride's veil and train in ceremony									■			■						
Accompany bride at altar									■									
Hold bride's bouquet during ceremony									■									

TABLE 15-2. WEDDING CEREMONY RESPONSIBILITIES (concluded)

■ = Primary
O = Optional

	Bride	Bride's Family	Bride's Mother	Bride's Father	Groom	Groom's Family	Groom's Mother	Groom's Father	Maid/Matron of Honor	Brides-maids	Junior Brides-maids	Best Man	Grooms-men	Junior Grooms-men	Flower Girl	Ring Bearer	Page/Train Bearer	Guest
Hold and pass groom's ring									■									
Sign marriage certificate/license									■			■						
Arrange transportation to ceremony												■						■
Serve as groom's aide												■						
Act as wedding chief of staff												■						
Oversee ushers												■						
Hold and pass bride's ring												■						
Hold marriage license												■						
Hold clergy/officiant fee												■						
Help groom dress												■						
Instruct and watch over ring bearer												■						
Wait with groom before ceremony												■						
Accompany groom at altar												■						
Ensure men's rental attire is returned												■						
Seat guests and honored guests at ceremony													■	O				
Light candles													O	O				
Lay aisle carpet													O	O				
Attach/remove aisle ribbons													O	O				
Escort honor guests after ceremony													■					
Act as escort for bridesmaids													■					
Provide bridesmaids' transportation to reception													O					
Act as escort for junior bridesmaids														■				
Carry flowers															■			
Carry ring pillow																■		
Carry bride's wedding dress train																	■	
Respond to wedding invitation																		■
Arrive on time at ceremony																		■
Stand for bride's entrance																		■
Follow bride's family lead during ceremony																		■
Remain seated for recessional																		■
Pass along receiving line																		■

CHAPTER 16

What Do the Ushers Do?

You may approach the usher situation in one of two ways: you may have your groomsmen be ushers, or you may have a separate group of men be ushers. It can be very convenient to have your groomsmen double as ushers. There are fewer people to keep track of, and the groomsmen are dressed similarly and well. But there may be males whom you haven't asked to be groomsmen, but would still like to include in your wedding. Asking them to be ushers creates several more male roles for your wedding party.

Depending upon the size and style of the wedding, the ushers can play a significant role. Being an usher can be a nerve-racking experience, particularly for someone who has never been an usher before.

At the rehearsal, the emphasis is on the wedding party movements and actions. The time before the wedding is a beehive of last-minute activities. As a result, there may not be much time devoted to explaining to the ushers what their responsibilities are.

One of the most important aspects of a wedding is that all the participants understand and feel comfortable with their assigned roles. To this end, the following instructions list the procedures for seating guests and the other special duties of the ushers. It is important that the ushers familiarize themselves with these instructions ahead of time. Any questions that may arise should be discussed with the clergy / officiant during the rehearsal or before the ceremony.

◻ General Duties

■ *Preparation*

❑ Try on tuxedo/attire before the service to make sure the garments fit and that all the parts are together.

❑ Pin the boutonniere on the left lapel.

❑ Arrive approximately forty-five minutes to one hour before the ceremony.

■ *Seating*

❑ The left side is reserved for friends and relatives of the bride.

❑ The right side is reserved for friends and relatives of the groom.

Note: *When there is no center aisle but rather two side aisles instead, the bride's friends and relatives are seated on both sides of the left aisle and the groom's friends and relatives on both sides of the right aisle.*

Note: *The seating is reversed in a Jewish wedding. The bride's friends and relatives are on the right side and the groom's are on the left.*

❑ Wait for guests on the left side of the entryway.

❑ Greet guests and initiate pleasant conversation with them if necessary. When talking with guests, use a low voice.

❑ Inquire about special pew cards issued to important guests, if such cards are used.

❑ Ask each woman guest where she prefers to sit, then offer your right arm and escort her to her seat.

❑ If several women guests arrive together without male escorts, escort the eldest woman to her seat first.

❑ If several couples arrive together, escort the eldest woman and have the other couples follow. The couples are then seated together.

❑ When guests arrive with children, the children follow.

Small children are not escorted.

❑ Men arriving alone are escorted to their seats but are not offered your arm except when the man is elderly and/or needs assistance; walk beside a single man on his left.

❑ Pause at the end of the aisle facing the escorted guests until the guests takes his/her seats; then return to the entryway to await the arrival of other guests.

❑ *No* loud talking; *no* gum chewing; *no* alcoholic beverages; *no* strong-smelling cologne.

❑ Be prepared to direct guests to parking areas, rest rooms, and the reception site.

❑ No one is seated by the usher after the bride's mother has been escorted to her place.

■ *Ceremony* (If the ushers are also the groomsmen)

❑ Line up for the processional in front of the bride and her party (unless entering with the groom and best man).

❑ During the ceremony, watch the bride arrive, hold your hands crossed in front, and do not lock your knees.

■ *After Ceremony*

❑ Escort bridesmaids during recessional (for groomsmen doubling as ushers).

❑ Return after the recessional to escort long-time and/or distinguished friends of the couple to the receiving line.

❑ Gather with the wedding party at the altar area for photographs (groomsmen and ushers).

❑ Make sure all the guests (with their belongings) have left before you leave.

❒ Special Duties

These are optional duties which the ushers *may* be asked to perform, depending on the size and style of the ceremony.

❑ Light the candles at the designated time (optional) and

extinguish them after the ceremony.

❑ Lay the aisle carpet/runner before the ceremony (normally after the bride's mother has been seated) and remove it after the ceremony (optional).

❑ Attach the aisle ribbons before the ceremony and remove them after the ceremony (optional).

❐ Head Usher — Special Assignments

❑ Make sure the other ushers arrive on time.

❑ Make certain that the best man, the groom, the groomsmen, and the other ushers are wearing their boutonnieres, that their coats are buttoned, and that they are all properly attired.

❑ Obtain special seating instructions for the seating of guests in the reserved section from the bride's mother and inform the other ushers of these seating instructions.

❑ Watch for uniform seating.

❑ Signal the organist/musicians when the processional is ready to start.

❐ Head Usher — Special Escorts

🕐 *Seven to ten minutes before the ceremony — groom's family*

❑ Escort the groom's great-grandmothers (father's side, then mother's side) to their places in the second row to the right of the altar.

❑ Escort the groom's grandmothers (father's side, then mother's side) to their places in the second row to the right of the altar.

❑ Escort the groom's mother to her place in the first row to the right of the altar.

🕐 *Three to six minutes before the ceremony — bride's family*

❑ Escort the bride's great-grandmothers (father's side,

then mother's side) to their places in the second row to the left of the altar.

❑ Escort the bride's grandmothers (father's side, then mother's side) to their places in the second row to the left of the altar.

Note: *Another option is to alternate the seating of the family members between the groom's and the bride's families, e.g. the groom's-great grandmother and then the bride's great-grandmother.*

🕐 *Two minutes before the ceremony*

❑ Escort the bride's mother to her place in the first row to the left of the altar.

Note: *When the bride's or groom's parents are divorced, normally the parent who raised the bride or groom is seated in the first row and the other parent is seated in the third row.*

Note: *When there is no center aisle but rather two side aisles instead, the parents are seated in the center section. The bride's parents are seated on the left and the groom's parents are seated on the right.*

Note: *In Jewish ceremonies, both the parents escort the bride and groom in the processional and are not seated by the ushers.*

Have We Talked?

Couples planning to marry are inclined to overempha-size the reception, decorations, apparel, prewedding parties, and photographs. In many cases, little attention is given to counseling preparation, contents of the ceremony, and the sig-nificance of marriage. Marriage is one of the most important commitments we make in our lifetime. It is one of the most rewarding, yet demanding, commitments you will make. You will experience a profound change in roles, relationships, and identities.

As a couple, you bring two unique ways of thinking and responding into the marriage relationship. You will have to make complicated and conflict-prone choices that will shape the direction of your lives. You must be open, patient, cre-ative, and flexible with each other in order to successfully learn the process of sharing and harmonizing your lives together.

You should realize that life is a series of stages. We come to the end of one stage and progress into another, such as ending our single lives and entering into marriage. Our past experiences impact how we approach and accomplish these transitions. Based upon our previous experiences, we develop certain attitudes and expectations and look to the future with either hope and anticipation or insecurity and fear. These experiences and expectations can either help or hinder the new relationship you are trying to build for a healthy, loving, mutually enriching marriage. This question-naire will help you develop a mutual understanding of what each other's expectations, duties and obligations, and rights and privileges in the marriage relationship are.

Falling in love is just the start of a marriage relationship. Loving marriage relationships do not just happen; they take constant care and nurturing. Likewise, a wedding ceremony lasts only a short time while a marriage is for a lifetime. Before entering into marriage, it is important to frankly and openly discuss as many marriage relationship issues as possible. This will ensure that your decision to marry is a sound one.

◻ Goals

Working through the following questionnaire will challenge you to communicate openly and honestly. It will provide you with the opportunity to seriously discuss the important spiritual, emotional, practical, and physical aspects of your marriage.

It will also help you to enrich your personal commitments to yourselves, to each other, to the marriage, and to God. It encourages you to strengthen your communication skills; evaluate priorities, values, and lifestyles; resolve irritations and conflicts; and deepen the intimacy of your relationship.

◻ Time Required

If used as part of your premarital counseling, you may be expected to attend one preliminary interview for you and your clergy member to discuss your wedding plans. The initial interview can be followed by additional meetings with the clergy member and/or a premarital counseling course conducted by the clergy member or trained lay instructors. The additional premarital counseling sessions normally range from three to six sessions of forty-five minutes to one hour each.

If it is not used as part of your premarital counseling, you may either complete the questionnaire on your own and compare your answers together or share the information with your clergy member. You should set aside approximately four to six hours for preparation time and discussion. However, this does not have to be accomplished all at one time. You may break the questionnaire down into sections as long as you make it a priority to schedule a regular time for the sessions. If the do-it-yourself method does not work, ask for help from your clergy member or seek out a trained marriage/family counselor.

❏ Materials

No special materials or supplies are required except for the questionnaire and a pen.

❏ Physical Setting

You should be in a warm, friendly, comfortable, informal, private setting where you can think about and openly discuss the questions undisturbed. The setting should be arranged so that you and your future spouse can be seated together to encourage positive, responsive, and caring discussion.

❏ Process

❑ Arrange an initial premarital interview with your clergy member to discuss the details of the wedding, to answer any questions each of you and/or your clergy member may have relative to the service, and to schedule premarital counseling sessions.

❑ Review marriage questionnaire independently, develop your personal responses, and then compare your answers, looking for similarities and differences. Patterns of compatibility or incompatibility should be the basis of discussion, and your decisions should be seriously considered before getting married.

❑ Attend premarital counseling sessions and read any books that may be recommended.

MARRIAGE LIFESTYLE QUESTIONNAIRE

■ **General**

◆ How long have you known each other?_____

◆ How long have you been engaged?_____

◆ How did you meet?_____

◆ What attracted you to each other?_____

◆ Do you and your future spouse have the same temperament, education, and religious background?
☐ Yes ☐ No

◆ How soon do you plan to be married?_____

◆ Are the two of you living together? ☐ Yes ☐ No
a. If so, for how long?_____

b. Why did you choose to live together?_____

c. What effect does living together have on your attitudes and expectations of marriage?_____

◆ Why marriage at this time?_____

◆ Do you love each other? ☐ Yes ☐ No

If yes, what do you think "love" means to you?_____

_____

◆ What led you to the decision to marry?_____

a. Have you recently experienced a major loss/gain?
☐ Yes ☐ No

b. Do you hate being alone? ☐ Yes ☐ No

c. Do you need your future spouse in order to feel important, successful, or wanted? ☐ Yes ☐ No

◆ What factors led you to believe you can have a happy married life together?_____

- ◆ Have you been engaged before? ☐ Yes ☐ No

  a. Did it result in marriage? ☐ Yes ☐ No

  b. If not, why did the engagement end?_____

- ◆ What are your ideas concerning marriage, and what is your mental image of marriage?_____

- ◆ Do you understand the meaning of a marriage founded in your religion? ☐ Yes ☐ No

- ◆ Is there any impediment to your marriage that you know of? ☐ Yes ☐ No

- ◆ How will marriage make you a better person than you would be by remaining single?_____

- ◆ Do you consider marriage to be a lifelong commitment? ☐ Yes ☐ No

- ◆ Is there anything in marriage that you fear? ☐ Yes ☐ No

- ◆ Do you have any doubts about the marriage? ☐ Yes ☐ No

- ◆ Is divorce a possibility for you? ☐ Yes ☐ No

  a. Under what circumstances?_____

  b. How does your future spouse feel about your answer?_____

- ◆ Will you (the bride) take your fiancé's family name, retain your own name, or use a hyphenated combination of both of your surnames?_____

■ **Previously Married**

- ◆ Have either or both of you been married before? ☐ Yes ☐ No

  If so, how many times?_____

- How did the previous marriages end (death, divorce, annulment)?_____

- How long ago did your previous marriage end?_____
  a. If it ended through death, was the death of your spouse sudden or over an extended period of time?

  _____

  b. Was the death a result of natural causes? ☐ Yes ☐ No

- If the previous marriage ended through divorce or annulment, how long was the process?_____

  Was it amicable or bitter?_____

- What type of relationship do you have with your former spouse?_____

- Do you still have contact with your former spouse?

  ☐ Yes ☐ No

  If so, how frequently?_____

- How does your future spouse feel about your relationship with your former spouse?_____
  a. Will that affect your marriage? ☐ Yes ☐ No
  b. If so, how?

- Are there any children as a result of the previous marriage? ☐ Yes ☐ No
  a. If so, how many?_____
  b. What are their ages?_____
  c. Do you share custody of the children with your former spouse? ☐ Yes ☐ No

     If so, how frequently?_____

  d. How do you and your future spouse's children get along?_____

- Do you pay or receive spousal or child support?

  ☐ Yes ☐ No

  a. If so, for how much longer?_____

  b. How does your future spouse feel about that?_____

  _____

  c. Will the support payments cause any budgetary problems for your marriage? ☐ Yes ☐ No

  d. If so, how are you planning on handling these problems?_____

- If you both have children from previous marriages, how do they get along with each other?_____

  _____

- How do you feel your future spouse treats your children?_____

- Have you discussed your decision to marry with your children? ☐ Yes ☐ No

  a. If so, what was their reaction?_____

  b. If not, when and how are you going to?_____

  _____

- Do your children support your marriage? ☐ Yes ☐ No

  a. If not, what impact will that have upon your relationship with your spouse?_____

  _____

  b. What impact will that have upon your relationship with his/her children?_____

  _____

- Where will your children stay during your honeymoon?_____

- Do your children's grandparents (your former spouse's parents) know of and support your marriage?

  ☐ Yes ☐ No

  If not, what impact will that have upon your relationship with your children?_____

- How will your experiences from the previous marriage affect your upcoming marriage, both positively and negatively?_____

  _____

- Based upon your experiences in the previous marriage, what are your expectations for your upcoming marriage?_____

  What are your apprehensions?_____

■ **Personal Attitudes**

- What do you like about each other?_____

- Do you like the same foods, colors, furniture styles?
  ☐ Yes ☐ No

- What is your future spouse's strongest point?_____

  _____

  Weakest?_____

- What does your future spouse do that irritates you?

  _____

- When have you experienced romance or disillusionment in your relationship?_____

- What specific changes would you like to see the other make after you are married?_____

a. Can you accept your partner without those changes?
☐ Yes ☐ No

b. How does your partner feel about those changes?
_____

• Are you jealous of your future spouse? ☐ Yes ☐ No
a. If so, why?_____
b. In what ways?_____

• What are your expectations of your roles in marriage?
a. Role of the wife?_____
b. Role of the husband?_____
c. How do you and your future spouse's concepts differ?_____

• What do you expect out of your marriage?
a. What do you expect to get?_____
b. What do you expect to give?_____

• What is the best thing that ever happened to you?
_____

The worst?_____

• What person had the greatest influence on your life and why?_____

■ **Ambitions and Goals**

• What is really important to you in life?_____

• What do you want to do more than anything else?
_____

• What goals are you seeking to achieve?_____
_____

How do you plan to achieve them?_____

_____

• What goals have you attempted to accomplish in life to date?_____

Which of these goals have you successfully accomplished, and which have you not?_____

_____

• How important is your career to you, and how important is your future spouse's career to you?_____

_____

• What are your personal and professional ambitions?

_____

a. How is your career/employment going to affect your marriage?_____

b. Will your future spouse work? ☐ Yes ☐ No

• What are your short-term employment objectives?

_____

Long-term?_____

• What is your attitude about relocating for future spouse's or your own career/ employment?_____

_____

• Do you have any mutual long-range goals? ☐ Yes ☐ No

a. In what ways are they different?_____

b. How are you going to resolve the differences?_____

_____

• What are your plans for obtaining future education/training?_____

• Are your home life plans compatible? ☐ Yes ☐ No

■ **Religion**

  • Were you reared in a religious home? ☐ Yes ☐ No

  • What is your religious background?_____

    a. If different from your fiancé's/fiancée's, have either of you considered joining your fiancé's/fiancée's church? ☐ Yes ☐ No

    b. Have you settled this issue yet? ☐ Yes ☐ No

  • How would you describe your current relationship with God?_____

  • Are you satisfied with your concept of God? ☐ Yes ☐ No

    a. Do you think your concept will change after the marriage? ☐ Yes ☐ No

    b. If so, how?_____

  • What are your plans for your religious life?_____

  _____

    a. What place does religion have in your life now?

    _____

    b. What place will it have in the future?_____

  • What level of religious commitment do you think your fiancé/fiancée has?_____

  • What are you doing and what will you do to encourage mutual emotional/spiritual growth in your relationship?_____

  • Are you sharing spiritual/religious experiences with your fiancé/fiancée? ☐ Yes ☐ No

  • Do you foresee any areas of conflict on spiritual issues? ☐ Yes ☐ No

- Who will be responsible for spiritual leadership in your home?_____

■ Communication

- When you are together, do you give each other your undivided attention? ☐ Yes ☐ No

   a. Do you really listen to each other? ☐ Yes ☐ No

   a. Are you sensitive to each other's feelings and aware of each other's needs? ☐ Yes ☐ No

- Can you discuss your deepest thoughts, interests, and concerns with each other? ☐ Yes ☐ No

- What things about yourself (thoughts, feelings, actions, fantasies) do you find difficult to reveal to and/or share with your fiancé/fiancée?_____

- Are there subjects that you can discuss more freely with others than with your future spouse?

   ☐ Yes ☐ No

- Do you trust someone else more than you do your future spouse? ☐ Yes ☐ No

- Who does the most talking when you are alone with each other?_____

- Are you or your fiancé/fiancée constantly trying to manipulate the other? ☐ Yes ☐ No

- Do you have a sense of humor? ☐ Yes ☐ No

   Does your future spouse? ☐ Yes ☐ No

- What kind of disagreements have you had?_____

   _____

- When you become bothered about something, how do

you react?_____

* How do you let your fiancé/fiancée know that you are angry?_____

* How do you settle disagreements?_____

* How do you feel about compromise?_____

  Are you willing to compromise when you cannot reach a mutual decision? ☐ Yes ☐ No

■ **Friends and Recreation**

* Do you have the same interests, hobbies, and amusements? ☐ Yes ☐ No

* What do you do during your time together?_____

  _____

  a. Apart?_____

  b. Who decides?_____

* Do you like each other's friends? ☐ Yes ☐ No

* How do you think your respective friendships will change after your marriage?_____

* What qualities and interests are you looking for in new friends?_____

* What can you, as a couple, do to make new friends?

  _____

* What organizations do you belong to?_____

  _____

■ **Finances**

* What are your financial goals?_____

  Are they compatible? ☐ Yes ☐ No

- How much income will you need to have the lifestyle you want?_____

- Do you know what your total gross/net income will be? ☐ Yes ☐ No

- Have you planned a tentative budget? ☐ Yes ☐ No

- What are your plans relative to saving?_____

- Who will handle the checkbook?_____

  Will you have joint savings/checking accounts or maintain separate accounts?_____

- What kind of insurance protection do you think you will need?_____

- Do you have any outstanding debts? ☐ Yes ☐ No
  What are your feelings about debts?_____
  _____

■ Residence

- Where will you live?_____

  In close proximity to in-laws? ☐ Yes ☐ No

- Where would you like to live?_____

  Why?_____

- Do you know and agree upon what type of home you want and can afford? ☐ Yes ☐ No

- How will you share the home maintenance chores?
  _____

■ Health

- Are you aware of any disease or disability, particularly

hereditary conditions, that might affect your future?
☐ Yes ☐ No

• Do you know the state law concerning blood tests and marriage license requirements? ☐ Yes ☐ No

• Have you ever been under treatment for emotional problems? ☐ Yes ☐ No

• What does abusive behavior mean to you?_____

_____

   a. Do you believe that you have ever exhibited abusive behavior? ☐ Yes ☐ No

   b. Have you ever physically or psychologically abused anyone? ☐ Yes ☐ No

• Are you currently using alcohol and/or recreational drugs? ☐ Yes ☐ No

   a. Have you ever used them in the past? ☐ Yes ☐ No

   b. What are your attitudes about alcohol/drug abuse?

_____

   c. Are those attitudes shared by your future spouse?
   ☐ Yes ☐ No

• Have you ever been treated for alcohol and/or drug dependency? ☐ Yes ☐ No

• Do you engage in healthy behavior? ☐ Yes ☐ No

   a. What is your attitude of a healthy lifestyle?_____

_____

   b. Is that attitude shared by your future spouse?
   ☐ Yes ☐ No

• Does your future spouse have any health or hygiene habits that irritate you? ☐ Yes ☐ No

   a. If so, what?_____

b. Have you made him/her aware of them? ☐ Yes ☐ No

■ **Sexual Relations**

- What are your attitudes about sex?_____

_____

Do you look forward to sex in your marriage?

☐ Yes ☐ No

- What qualities of your future spouse do you find sexually attractive?_____

- Do you know of any reason why you could not have a normal sex life?_____

- Are you and your future spouse sexually active at this time? ☐ Yes ☐ No

- Have you discussed what you each enjoy sexually? (Or, if not sexually active, what you think you *will* enjoy.)

_____

a. In what ways are your responses different?_____

_____

b. How are you going to resolve the differences?_____

_____

- Have you told one another about previous sexual relations, if any? ☐ Yes ☐ No
  a. If so, have you accepted that fact about each other? ☐ Yes ☐ No
  b. If not, will you be able to? ☐ Yes ☐ No

- How do you feel your previous sexual encounters will affect your marriage?_____

- Are there any sexual acts that you think are improper in marriage? ☐ Yes ☐ No

a. If so, what?_____

Why?_____

b. Does your future spouse share your feelings?
☐ Yes ☐ No

♦ What will happen if you discover one partner is more demanding sexually than the other?_____

_____

♦ Do you know the difference between sex (physical relationship) and love (emotional relationship)? ☐ Yes ☐ No

a. If so, what is the difference?_____

b. Does your future spouse share your feelings?
☐ Yes ☐ No

♦ Have you read any books on the physical aspects of marriage? ☐ Yes ☐ No

Or on marriage in general? ☐ Yes ☐ No

■ Child Rearing

♦ Do you both want children? ☐ Yes ☐ No

a. When?_____

b. How many?_____

♦ If you cannot have children, what are your attitudes about infertility assistance (in vitro fertilization, donor insemination, adoption)?_____

♦ If you do not want children, have you discussed birth control? ☐ Yes ☐ No

♦ If you are planning or are now using birth control, is the method satisfactory to both of you? ☐ Yes ☐ No

♦ What do you believe the involvement of the husband should be in raising children?_____

The wife?_____

- What do you think about the "working mother" in relation to child rearing?_____

- What values do you want to instill in your children?
  _____

- What methods of discipline will you use with your children?_____

- Do you intend to impart religious beliefs and practices to your children? ☐ Yes ☐ No

  a. In what faith do you plan to raise your children?

  _____

  b. Does your future spouse share your intentions?
  ☐ Yes ☐ No

■ **Parent Relationship**

- Are/were you close to your family? ☐ Yes ☐ No

  How does your family feel about the marriage?

  _____

- How would you characterize your parents' relationship with each other?_____

- Which parent has the decision-making/leadership role?_____

- Do/did your parents openly show affection (i.e. hugging, kissing, using endearing words, complimenting each other frequently)? ☐ Yes ☐ No

- What is your assessment of your parents' happiness in marriage?_____

- What qualities in your parents' marriage would you like to duplicate in your marriage?_____

  What qualities would you like to avoid?_____

- What were your parents' goals in life?_____

  _____

  How well have they achieved them?_____
- How do your parents manage their finances?_____

  _____
- How do/did you see your parents' marriage affecting your concept of marriage?_____
- How do/did you treat your parents?_____
- Do you regard your parents as equals? ☐ Yes ☐ No
- Are either of you overly dependent on your parents? ☐ Yes ☐ No
- How did you get along with your siblings?_____

■ **In-Law Relationships**

- Do you get along with your future in-laws? ☐ Yes ☐ No

  a. What do you like about your future in-laws?

  _____

  b. What do you dislike?_____
- What do you believe your future in-laws' attitudes are about you?_____
- How do you believe your future in-laws feel about your pending marriage?
- What potential conflicts do you foresee with your future in-laws?_____
- How frequently will you be involved with your future in-laws?_____

❑ Encounter Groups

Even after discussing the above questions and partici-pating in the premarital counseling sessions with your clergy member, you still may find it advantageous to take part in an engaged encounter group tailored specifically for pre-married couples. These programs, normally conducted as weekend retreats, can strengthen and renew your relation-ship with each other. They give you an opportunity to share intimate feelings that you may find difficult to discuss at home, and to address issues that can make your relationship healthier and your marriage stronger.

Normally, you meet with a small group of engaged couples, under the leadership of trained counselors, to discuss your attitudes toward each other and your expecta-tions regarding such topics as marriage, family, and sexuality. You are afforded an opportunity to examine your ideals, goals, and desires.

There are many private and religious encounter group programs offered. You should investigate which program best meets your particular needs before committing your-selves to attend.

❑ Marriage Preparation Sessions

In addition to the engaged encounter groups, many churches, parishes, and synagogues offer (and many times require attendance in) regularly scheduled marriage prepara-tion sessions conducted by the clergy member or trained lay instructors. These are specifically designed group sessions to assist you in clarifying your expectations of marriage and to address your questions about married life.

ABOUT THE AUTHOR

STEVEN M. NEEL has officiated at weddings for twenty years. He also works within both the aerospace and criminal justice industries, where he is able to provide both technical assistance to his customers and pastoral counseling to his fellow employees and friends.

The Reverend Doctor Neel received a B.S. in criminology from California State University at Long Beach and an MPA in public administration from the University of Southern California. He attended a non-denominational seminary, the Humanity Research Center of Beverly Hills, where he received both a D.D. and certificate of ordination in 1976. He is currently enrolled in the Doctor of Philosophy (Church Administration) Program at Trinity College and Seminary. He is married and lives with his wife, Carmen, in San Jose, California.

NOTES

NOTES

ORDER FORM

MERIWETHER PUBLISHING LTD.
P.O. BOX 7710
COLORADO SPRINGS, CO 80933
TELEPHONE: (719) 594-4422

Please send me the following books:

_____ **Saying "I Do" #TT-B122**   **$10.95**
by Steven M. Neel
A complete guide to a perfect wedding

_____ **Wedding Vows #TT-B151**   **$10.95**
by Peg Kehret
How to express your love in your own words

_____ **Fund Raising for Youth #TT-B184**   **$9.95**
by Dorthy M. Ross
Hundreds of wonderful ways of raising funds for youth organizations

_____ **The Parents Book of Ballet #TT-B121**   **$10.95**
by Angela Whitehill and William Noble
A guide to the care and development of a young dancer

_____ **Absolutely Unforgettable Parties! #TT-B135**   **$9.95**
by Janet Litherland
Great ideas for party people

_____ **Clown Act Omnibus #TT-B118**   **$12.95**
by Wes McVicar
Everything you need to know about clowning

_____ **The Mime Book #TT-B124**   **$12.95**
by Claude Kipnis
A comprehensive guide to the art of mime

**These and other fine Meriwether Publishing books are available at
your local bookstore or direct from the publisher. Use the handy
order form on this page.**

NAME: _____

ORGANIZATION NAME: _____

ADDRESS: _____

CITY:_____ STATE: _____ ZIP: _____

PHONE: _____
  ❑ **Check Enclosed**
  ❑ **Visa or MasterCard #** _____

Signature: _____ *Expiration*
          Date: _____
(required for Visa/MasterCard orders)

COLORADO RESIDENTS: Please add 3% sales tax.
SHIPPING: Include $2.75 for the first book and 50¢ for each additional book ordered.

  ❑ *Please send me a copy of your complete catalog of books and plays.*

ORDER FORM

MERIWETHER PUBLISHING LTD.
P.O. BOX 7710
COLORADO SPRINGS, CO 80933
TELEPHONE: (719) 594-4422

Please send me the following books:

———————— **Saying "I Do" #TT-B122**   **$10.95**
by Steven M. Neel
A complete guide to a perfect wedding

———————— **Wedding Vows #TT-B151**   **$10.95**
by Peg Kehret
How to express your love in your own words

———————— **Fund Raising for Youth #TT-B184**   **$9.95**
by Dorthy M. Ross
Hundreds of wonderful ways of raising funds for youth organizations

———————— **The Parents Book of Ballet #TT-B121**   **$10.95**
by Angela Whitehill and William Noble
A guide to the care and development of a young dancer

———————— **Absolutely Unforgettable Parties! #TT-B135**   **$9.95**
by Janet Litherland
Great ideas for party people

———————— **Clown Act Omnibus #TT-B118**   **$12.95**
by Wes McVicar
Everything you need to know about clowning

———————— **The Mime Book #TT-B124**   **$12.95**
by Claude Kipnis
A comprehensive guide to the art of mime

**These and other fine Meriwether Publishing books are available at
your local bookstore or direct from the publisher. Use the handy
order form on this page.**

NAME: _____

ORGANIZATION NAME: _____

ADDRESS: _____

CITY:_____ STATE: _____ ZIP: _____

PHONE: _____
   ❑ **Check Enclosed**
   ❑ **Visa or MasterCard #** _____

Signature: _____   *Expiration
                                 Date:* _____
    (required for Visa/MasterCard orders)

COLORADO RESIDENTS: Please add 3% sales tax.
SHIPPING: Include $2.75 for the first book and 50¢ for each additional book ordered.

  ❑ *Please send me a copy of your complete catalog of books and plays.*